ECUMENICAL STUDIES IN WORSHIP
No. 6

THE PASCHAL LITURGY
AND
THE APOCALYPSE

by

MASSEY H. SHEPHERD, Jr.,
Ph.D., S.T.D., D.D.

Professor of Liturgics
Church Divinity School of the Pacific
Berkeley, California

JOHN KNOX PRESS
Richmond, Virginia
Library Congress Catalog Card No. 60-7041

ECUMENICAL STUDIES IN WORSHIP

General Editors:

J. G. DAVIES, M.A., D.D.
  Reader in Theology, The University of Birmingham
A. RAYMOND GEORGE, M.A., B.D.
  Tutor, Wesley College, Headingley, Leeds

Advisory Board:

PROFESSOR OSCAR CULLMANN
  Universities of Basel and the Sorbonne

PROFESSOR H. GRADY DAVIS
  Chicago Lutheran Seminary, U.S.A.

DR. F. W. DILLISTONE
  Dean of Liverpool Cathedral, England

PROFESSOR ROGER HAZLETON
  Pomona College, Claremont, California, U.S.A.

PROFESSOR J. KUMARESAN
  Gurukul Lutheran College, Madras, India

REV. R. STUART LOUDEN
  Kirk of the Greyfriars, Edinburgh

DR. ROBERT NELSON
  Dean, Theological Faculty, Vanderbilt University, U.S.A.

CANON D. R. VICARY
  Headmaster, King's School, Rochester, England

SHERMAN ELBRIDGE JOHNSON

AMICO ET SOCIO
CARISSIMO

First published 1960

Copyright © 1960 Massey H. Shepherd, Jr.

Lutterworth Press
4 Bouverie Street, London, E.C.4

Printed in Great Britain by
Latimer, Trend & Co., Ltd., Plymouth

CONTENTS

ABBREVIATIONS

ATR   *Anglican Theological Review*

BC   *The Beginnings of Christianity*, edited by F. J. Foakes Jackson
        and Kirsopp Lake, 5 vols., 1920–33

HTR   *The Harvard Theological Review*

JBL   *The Journal of Biblical Literature*

JTS   *The Journal of Theological Studies*

ThWb *Theologisches Wörterbuch zum Neuen Testament*, edited by
        Gerhard Kittel, 1933–

ZNTW *Zeitschrift für die neutestamentliche Wissenschaft und die Kunde
        des Urchristentums*

Part One

THE PASCHAL LITURGY
IN THE PRIMITIVE CHURCH

I

THE APOSTOLIC AGE

(A) THE DAY

OUR KNOWLEDGE of the beginnings of Christian worship depends upon a summary statement in the Book of Acts describing the communal life of the primitive Church in Jerusalem:

> They were constant in the teaching of the Apostles and the fellowship, in the breaking of bread and the prayers. . . . And being daily in attendance with one accord in the Temple, and breaking bread from house to house, they took their food, in gladness and simplicity of heart praising God and having favor with all the people. (2: 42, 46.)

To what extent the Evangelist is here recording from his sources, or is interpreting his sources in the light of his own later experience, we cannot tell. He is, however, an author who does not play fast and loose with documentary sources, as one may attest from his use of Mark in his gospel narratives. In this passage he may depend not on a written document, but on oral tradition.

Certainly the "breaking of bread" refers to a cultic act, the Eucharist or Eucharist-Agape of the Church. It is not taken to be an ordinary meal, for it is one of a list of four terms pointing to corporate religious worship and activity. And secondly, it is mentioned as co-ordinate with daily attendance in the Temple. The phrases "to break bread" or "the breaking of bread" were not used in Jewish or Hellenistic sources to describe a meal as a whole, but referred only to a single action at a meal. Christian usage alone employed the phrases as a technical reference to the Church's cultic meal. The author of Acts uses it thus in 20: 7, 11; and it probably bears the same meaning in Luke 24: 30, less certainly so in Acts 27: 35. St. Paul speaks of "the bread which we break" in 1 Corinthians 10: 16 definitely of the eucharistic bread. Similarly in the *Didache* 14: 1 and in Ignatius' letter to the Ephesians

20: 2, "to break bread" is unmistakably a cultic reference to the Eucharist.[1]

The Latin, Coptic, and Syriac Peshitto versions of Acts 2: 42 explicitly place "the breaking of bread and the prayers" in apposition to "the fellowship". This exegesis is possible, though unnecessary. The word "fellowship" or "communion" (κοινωνία) embraced more than a sharing in or participation in sacrament and prayer, though St. Paul, again in 1 Corinthians 10: 16, used it precisely of the Church's sharing in the Body and Blood of Christ.[2] In the present context in Acts, the fellowship-communion with the Apostles must also have included the sharing of common goods by the members of the Church, and their distribution to each according to need. A concrete illustration of it is denoted in Acts 6: 1 ff. in the daily "ministry" to the widows of the community from the common tables of the Church. It does not matter whether this serving of tables refers to the cultic meal or to economic administration. The Church's worship and charity were in any case closely linked. Dr. Joachim Jeremias is bold enough to suggest that the four notes of the Church's corporate life listed in Acts 2: 42 outline the sequence of a service of worship, in which case the "fellowship" is a reference to the offering.[3]

It seems evident that the cultic eucharistic meal of the primitive Jerusalem church was a *daily* celebration. Not only is this suggested by the comparison with daily attendance in the Temple, but also by the notice in Acts 6: 1 of daily distribution of charity to the widows from the Church's tables. It would be absurd, of course, to question how a religious community of three thousand persons, shortly increased to five thousand with daily accessions of membership, could be accommodated in a house-church cultic meal in the crowded living quarters of Jerusalem. The Evangelist is as little concerned with problems created by his statistics as were the editors of the Pentateuch with the feeding and sheltering of the multitudes of Hebrew pilgrims in the wilderness. He leaves to his reader an imaginative reconstruction of the

[1] See J. Behm, *ThWb* III, 727–9; J. Jeremias, *The Eucharistic Words of Jesus*, 1955, pp. 82–4; O. Cullmann, *Early Christian Worship*, 1953, pp. 14–15; P. H. Menoud, "Les Actes des Apôtres et l'Eucharistie", *Revue d'histoire et de philosophie religieuses* XXXIII, 1953, pp. 23–6. Cf. also Foakes Jackson and K. Lake, *BC* IV, 28.

[2] The word *koinonia*, of course, has even wider connotations in NT usage. See F. Hauck, *ThWb* III, 798–810; H. Seesemann, *Der Begriff KOINΩNIA im Neuen Testament* (Beihefte zur ZNTW 14), 1933; J. Y. Campbell, "KOINΩNIA and its Cognates in the New Testament", *JBL* LI, 1932, pp. 352–80; G. V. Jourdan, "KOINΩNIA in 1 Corinthians 10: 16", *ibid.* LXVII, 1948, pp. 111–24.

[3] *Op. cit.*, p. 83, n. 3.

"at home" or "house to house" assemblies (2: 46). One may picture the companies crowded into a single dwelling, or gathered in uncounted house-assemblies; or one may reconstruct a sequence of meetings in all parts of the city, from day to day, so as to provide a convenience of communication for converts all over Jerusalem. Only modern historians worry about such numerical problems. The author of Acts was concerned only to testify to the fulfilment of God's purpose in the spread of the gospel of salvation.

Actually, one comprehends the life and worship of this primitive Christian community only as one recognizes in the narrative of Acts how it is manifested simultaneously at two levels, or rather two realms of existence: that of time, and that of beyond-time. Its members, who are still Jews, albeit Jews with a new understanding of the Old Testament, remain within the historic framework of Israel's institutionalized religion. They obey its laws and worship in its ordered cultus of daily sacrifice, weekly Sabbath, and annual fast and festival. Indeed, the Apostles are depicted as observing, with the most pious of their Jewish brethren, the daily ordering of "hours of prayer" in the Temple (3: 1). But their interest in the Temple is something more than a place of resort for pious exercises. It is the principal locus of proclamation of the exaltation of Jesus, "whom the heaven must receive until the times of establishing all that God spoke by the mouth of his holy prophets from of old" (3: 21). Nor was this selection of the Temple as a daily place of resort solely pragmatic, since it was the most obvious place in Jerusalem for men with a message to reach the attention of the largest and most diverse number of people. The Temple was also the place of expectation of the imminent return of the Lord from heaven, according to the prophet's warning: "The Lord, whom ye seek, shall suddenly come to his temple, even the messenger of the covenant, whom ye delight in" (Malachi 3: 1). In view of such expectation the Jewish cultus and observance had but transitory significance, for its end was near.

So the peculiar worship of the newly constituted Israel in Christ—that which was celebrated "from house to house"—was revelation of "the last times", the times of the pouring out of God's Spirit of the Lord. In the context of this inbreaking of "the last days" the Christian house-gatherings for the breaking of bread were real anticipations of the Messianic banquet shortly to be consummated in the final end of the age. This assurance was rooted in the institution and promise of the Last Supper and actualized in the living presence of the Risen Lord when He was "made known to them in the breaking of bread" on Easter Day. The New Covenant rite stands in between the redemptive event of Cross and Resurrection and the redemptive fulfilment of the Second Coming. Though it is in time, it is in a truer sense beyond time. Dr. Oscar Cullmann is surely right in his insistence upon this eschatological tension realized in the Church's Supper, and in his emphasis upon the acclamation cry *Maranatha*, "Our Lord, come!", as expressive of the true character of this worship. It is both "Come to us who are assembled in thy name", and "Come finally at the end".[1]

The eucharistic meal is thus not tied to a time of observance, but is characteristic of whenever, wherever the Church assembles as Church. It is daily not because of a legal enactment, like the daily sacrifices of the Temple. Nor is it yet (though it is soon to be) associated with a weekly assembly, like the synagogue service. Much less is it an annual festival. For this reason, one may hazard the conjecture that the much disputed point as to whether the Last Supper of Jesus was actually a Passover meal may never be resolved. Either it was a very much transformed Passover or it was a new substitution for the Passover. For the Supper is not so much a rite of historical commemoration, though it is that; it is a rite of historical fulfilment. It is not an annual remembrance only of what God has done, but a present, constant experience of what God has done and will do. Its context is urgent, immediate, like the petition of the Lord's Prayer: Give us for the day—or, it may be, for the morrow—our bread. But it is only for the day, for who can foretell the coming of the final Day?

One understands, in this perspective, the crucial character of the later controversy with the Quartodecimans. However apostolic the Quartodeciman observance may have been in origin, or however sincerely transformed with Christian meaning the character of its celebration, it was rightly suspected by the majority of the Church as a Judaizing practice. For it tied the celebration of the redemptive event within the time-framework of the old Law. The judgment of Hippolytus upon Quartodecimanism was just:

> They have regard only to that which has been written in the Law. . . . They pay no attention to the fact that it was enacted for the Jews, who were to kill the true Passover. And this (*i.e.* the Pascha) has spread to the Gentiles and is discerned by faith, not kept strictly in the letter.[2]

For similar reasons, it can not be determined with historical exactitude whether the command to repeat the Supper, "Do this in remem-

---

[1] *Christ and Time*, 1950, pp. 155–6; also his *Early Christian Worship*, pp. 13–20.
[2] *Philosophumena* viii, 18. See below, pp. 46–7.

brance of me," is authentic. It is true to the realities of the situation if it is seen in relation to the interim or intermediate period between Resurrection and Second Coming, whether it be in actual time count one day or thousands of years. It is not true if it is conceived as a legal (or even rubrical) directive of a new law for an historic institution. For it lacks precisely a clear enunciation of "how often" or "just when" the Supper is to be repeated. The evidence of St. Paul is decisive at this point, even though the apostle, when writing First Corinthians, was already familiar not only with this command to repeat, but also with a weekly ordering of the Church's assembly on Sundays. But in recalling the Last Supper he does not tie it to Passover or to any calendar day, but identifies it as regards time solely by "the night in which he was betrayed". And in his explanation of both the command to repeat and the meaning of what is repeated, he says only: "For *as often* as you eat this bread and drink the cup, you proclaim the Lord's death *until he comes*" (1 Cor. 11: 26).

(B) THE WEEK

The daily celebration of the eucharistic meal gave way, within the apostolic period, to a weekly observance. The process of this development may not have taken place uniformly; we have no records of the stages that marked this change. Only the fact is established, from two quite independent sources, that within a generation of the death and resurrection of Jesus the normative time of gathering of the Christian Churches took place "on the first day of the week". St. Paul, in 1 Corinthians 16: 2, attests to this Sunday meeting in his directives concerning the offering that he committed himself to gather for the "poor" in Jerusalem. The "we-source" of Acts 20: 7 is more explicit: "on the first day of the week when we were gathered together to break bread".

In regard to the latter reference, questions have been raised whether the service took place on Saturday evening or Sunday evening. If Jewish reckoning of the day from sunset to sunset is meant, then the assembly took place on Saturday evening. It is important to bear in mind this Jewish method of counting the days, for it has left in later Christian liturgy unmistakable relics in the way the "eves" of festivals have been accounted as belonging to the festival observance itself. But the author of Acts generally follows the Hellenistic custom of reckoning the day from morning to morning. And in the context of the passage under consideration he notes Paul's intention of leaving "on the morrow" at daybreak, which would be Monday. We may leave the matter open, noting only that the Evangelist's source may have implied the Jewish day-reckoning but that it was understood by the Evangelist according to his own manner and custom. In any case, the gathering on the first day of the week is introduced as a customary one. It was not an extraordinary meeting simply because of a farewell visit by the apostle.[1]

The transfer from a daily to a weekly celebration should not be taken as due to any dimming of the expectation of the Parousia of the Lord. It can be explained solely on practical grounds. The growth of the Church both in numbers and in geographical extent, the incorporation of Gentiles no less than Jews within the fellowship, and the evangelization of all sorts of people in all types of occupation—these factors alone would make a daily gathering of Christians impossible, if the unity of the Church and the full participation of all its members in its cultic acts were to be maintained.

The adoption of the weekly cycle of Sunday eucharistic worship was not an invention or a peculiarity of Gentile Christians, either in imitation of the Jewish Sabbath or in response to the "international astrology" that began to popularize the planetary week throughout the Roman Empire from the time of Augustus.[2] Certainly the Church adopted the week from Judaism, counting the days numerically as did the Jews, but denoting Friday as the Preparation and Saturday as the Sabbath. (This method is still followed in the Greek and Latin liturgical books.) There is evidence, albeit late, that is in Eusebius, that the Jewish Christians observed not only the Sabbath, but also Sunday; but this information may be of worth only with respect to those Jewish Christians who maintained communion with Gentile Christians.[3]

One may surmise that the Church's adoption of a weekly celebration came out of its evangelistic mission in the synagogues, where Moses and the prophets "were read every Sabbath" (cf. Acts 13: 27; 15: 21). We may suppose that the early Christian missionaries, after gathering a nucleus of converts from Jews and Gentile god-fearers who attended the synagogue Sabbath worship, assembled them in the house-churches on Saturday evening, when the Sabbath was over, for their peculiar Christian supper-rite. Thus Jewish converts would remain undisturbed

---

[1] Jackson and Lake, *BC* IV, 255; C. Callewaert, "La synaxe eucharistique à Jérusalem berceau du dimanche", *Ephemerides Theologicae Lovaniensis* XV, 1938, pp. 34–47; C. Marcora, *La vigilia nella liturgia* (Archivio Ambrosiano VI), 1954, pp. 24–9.

[2] F. H. Colson, *The Week*, 1926, p. 59.

[3] Eusebius *H.E.* iii, 27, 5. Cf. H. J. Schoeps, *Theologie und Geschichte des Judenchristentums*, 1949, p. 139, who believes that it was "not impossible" that heretical Jewish-Christians also observed Sunday.

in their accustomed way of observing the Sabbath. And Gentiles, who reckoned the day not from sunset to sunset but from sunrise to sunrise, might still view the Saturday evening meeting as in some sense a sharing in the Sabbath observance. As the primitive Church in Jerusalem followed its daily attendance in the Temple with its daily house-to-house Eucharist, after the Temple rites for the day were over; so the mission churches would follow attendance at the synagogue on the Sabbath by the house celebrations of the Lord's Supper, when the Sabbath was past. It is at least worth noting that neither St. Paul nor the "we-source" of Acts as yet spoke of a "Lord's day". They used the Jewish terminology: the first day of the week.

Such a reconstruction remains, nonetheless, purely hypothetical. It can neither be affirmed nor denied from the extant evidence. According to Acts, the first preaching of the gospel in the synagogue took place in Jerusalem, with the disputations of Stephen with leaders and members of the Greek-speaking synagogues in the holy city. In the tradition of Stephen's preaching, there is no suggestion that he viewed the Christian cult to be in any way an extension or transposition of the Jewish rites of worship. On the contrary, Stephen attacked the most cherished institutions of Judaism: the holy land, the Law, and the Temple. Though his speech of defense contained no particular polemic against the Sabbath, it may very well have involved this issue, for the formal charges laid against him were that "this Jesus of Nazareth will destroy this place and will change the customs that Moses handed on to us" (Acts 6: 14).

The bitter controversy aroused in the apostolic Church by the zeal of the Judaizers centered chiefly in the questions of circumcision and the dietary laws. There is much less evidence of sharp debate about Sabbath-keeping. Yet observance of the Sabbath was as much a hallmark of Judaism as were these other two controverted issues. It may be that the Christian gatherings for worship, since they were held on a day other than the Sabbath, did not pose so painful a problem to Jewish conscience. It was not the day of observance that troubled the Judaizers, but the promiscuous participation in a common meal by both circumcised and uncircumcised believers. Nonetheless, the problem of the Sabbath could not be ignored. The Gentile convert in being freed from the obligation of the Law was freed thereby from the keeping of the Sabbath. In a strong warning to the Colossian Christians, St. Paul affirmed: "Let no one judge you in matters of food and drink, or with regard to a festival or a new moon or a sabbath" (2: 16; cf. Gal. 4: 10). And, if we may trust the evidence of Acts, Jewish converts to Christianity were not suffered to remain long in good standing with their former synagogue confrères.

In any case, there is no evidence whatever in Christian sources of the apostolic or post-apostolic periods that the Church's observance of the Sunday Eucharist was ever considered to be either an extension of or a substitute for the Jewish law of the Sabbath. The adoption by the Church of the first day of the week rested upon neither example nor injunction of Jesus, nor, so far as is known, upon any apostolic decree or conciliar decision. When, by the end of the first century at the latest, the Church began to reflect upon what had happened, the name of the "Lord's day" was already a fixed usage throughout the Church.[1] And this Lord's day was extolled in the sharpest antithesis to the Jewish Sabbath. With intense conviction Ignatius of Antioch stated:

> If then those who lived by the ancient practices came to a new hope, by no longer keeping the Sabbath, but by living according to the Lord's day, on which also our life arose through Him and His death—though some deny this—through this mystery we received our faith; and because of it we suffer, in order that we may be found disciples of Jesus Christ our only Teacher.[2]

The key point to note in Ignatius' affirmation is that the keeping of the Sabbath and the living of the Lord's day are expressions that set in contrast Judaism and Christianity, respectively. And furthermore, the living of the Lord's day is an actualizing in the disciple of Jesus, even unto suffering, of the redemptive *mysterion* that has been accomplished in the death and resurrection of the Lord. The Lord's day celebration has now concentrated upon itself the same character and meaning as had those daily house-to-house celebrations in the primitive days of joyful expectation between the Resurrection and the Coming of the Lord. Only it is enriched by two generations of experience of fellowship and communion in His sufferings.

For one thing, the Church has become secure in its conviction, now that the Temple has been destroyed and its separation from the synagogue has been completed, that the Law of the old covenant, including the Sabbath, has served its transitory purpose and been fulfilled in Christ. Thus it understands the gospel traditions concerning the disputes of Jesus with the Jewish authorities about the keeping of the Sabbath. "I tell you that one greater than the Temple is here. For if you knew

---

[1] Rev. 1: 10; *Didache* 14, 1; Ignatius *Mag.* 9, 1; Dionysius of Corinth in Eusebius *H.E.* iv, 23, 11. Apologists to the heathen, such as Justin and Tertullian, often used, however, the pagan name of Sunday.

[2] *Mag.* 9, 1.

what it means, 'I desire mercy and not sacrifice,' you would not have condemned the innocent. For the Son of Man is Lord even of the Sabbath" (Matt. 12: 6–8). Christ is thus the reality which the Sabbath (as also the Temple) prefigured; or, to use St. Paul's words in the Colossians passage quoted above, "these things (i.e., festival and new moon and sabbath) are shadows of things to come, but the reality (lit. the body) belongs to Christ."

Writing to the mixed Jewish and Gentile church in Rome, St. Paul brought out in a remarkable way the new situation and context of Christian observances revealed in the death and resurrection of Christ. The honor given to one day is no different from the honor given to every day, provided only it is honored for the sake of the Lord. And the same principle applies to food, whatever food that is taken in *eucharistia*, thanksgiving to God:

> One man judges one day better than another, while another man judges every day alike. Let each one be fully convinced in his own mind. He who has regard for the day, regards it unto the Lord. Also he who eats, eats unto the Lord, since he gives thanks to God. And he who does not eat, does not eat unto the Lord, but gives thanks unto God. None of us lives unto himself, and none dies unto himself. For if we live, we live unto the Lord; and if we die, we die unto the Lord. Therefore, whether we live or die, we are the Lord's. To this end, Christ died and lives, in order that He might be Lord of the dead and the living (Rom. 14: 5–9).

The gospels provide another perspective upon the fulfilment of the Sabbath in Christ. It is noteworthy that St. Matthew precedes the narrative of Jesus' conflict with the Pharisees over keeping the Sabbath (cited above) by the proclamation: "Come unto me all ye who labor and are heavy laden, and I will give you rest" (11: 28). The true "rest" of the Sabbath is now revealed in Christ. The old creation is completed. The new creation is at the same time now at work. So, instead of God's rest, the Fourth Evangelist approaches a similar conflict between Jesus and the Jews with the concept of God's work. After the healing of the paralytic on the Sabbath, "the Jews persecuted Jesus, because he did this on the Sabbath. But Jesus answered them, 'My Father is working until now, and I am working' " (John 5: 17). Thus the rest of God in the work of creation, in so far as it is commemorated on the Sabbath, loses all significance. It is rather the re-creative, re-deeming work of God in His Son that makes all days point to a rest that is both achieved in Christ and yet to be consummated when Christ shall have reconciled all things to Himself and delivered the kingdom to the Father.[1] The comment of Origen upon the Johannine passage just quoted is illuminating:

> He shows by this that God does not on any Sabbath of this age rest from ordering the world or from dispensing His providence to the human race. For from the beginning He made creatures and created substances in such numbers as He the Creator of things knew could suffice for the perfection of the world, and He does not cease even unto the consummation of the age from His provision and ordering of them. But the true Sabbath, in which God shall rest from all His works, will be the future age when grief and sadness and anguish shall flee away, and God shall be all in all.[2]

The eschatological "rest" of the Sabbath was the object of an ingenious piece of exegesis of Psalm 95: 11 by the author of Hebrews (3: 7—4: 13). The rest of God upon the seventh day could not have referred to creation, since God had finished His works from the foundation of the world. Nor could it have referred to the historic rest of God's people in the land of Canaan, after the wilderness wandering, for there yet remained many who were hardened by disobedience. "Therefore there remains a sabbath rest for the people of God. . . . Let us strive then to enter into that rest."

The ground is thus laid for the post-apostolic interest in the typology of the numbers seven and eight (the octave), where is brought together the true relationship of history and eschatology, creation and final end, Sabbath and Sunday, as they are now understood through the death and Resurrection of Christ. The exegetical cue for this numbers-typology was the passage in Psalm 90: 4 that speaks of a thousand years as but a day in God's sight (cf. 2 Peter 3: 8). The seven days of the creation narrative of Genesis I were therefore taken to represent seven thousand years—the first six of them signifying the history of the world, the seventh or Sabbath representing the millennium that precedes the final judgment. The eighth day or octave, which begins a new week, opens the endless day of the age to come. But the eighth day is also the first day of the week, the day of the Resurrection of Christ, the day that foreshadows the final resurrection of the end of the world.

Neither the typology nor the millenarian doctrine based upon it

---

[1] For this entire section I am much indebted to J. Daniélou, *The Bible and the Liturgy*, 1956, pp. 222 ff. See also O. Cullmann, "Sabbat und Sonntag nach dem Johannesevangelium *Ἕως ἄρτι* (Joh. 5: 17)", *In Memoriam Ernst Lohmeyer*, ed. by W. Schmauch, 1951, pp. 127–31.

[2] *Hom. in Num.* xxiii, 4.

may appeal to modern taste. Yet its roots must go back to "apostolic tradition". It underlies the whole scheme of the vision of the triumph of Christ as it is laid out in the Book of Revelation—that vision which was revealed on the Lord's day, of which more will be said in detail in Part Two of this monograph. It is the tradition of "the elders who saw John, the disciple of the Lord", that Papias gathered so fervently in his *Interpretations of the Lord's Oracles* and passed on to Irenaeus.[1] It is likewise a tradition known to Justin Martyr, who accepted the Johannine and apostolic authorship of Revelation.[2] It was stated in its most succinct form in the post-apostolic, pseudo-Epistle of Barnabas 15:

> He speaks of the Sabbath at the beginning of creation: "And God made in six days the works of his hands, and on the seventh day he completed them and rested on it and sanctified it." . . .
>
> What does it mean that He completed them in six days? It means this: that the Lord will complete all things in six thousand years; for a day with Him signifies a thousand years. . . .
>
> "And he rested on the seventh day." This means: when His Son comes He will destroy the time of the wicked one and judge the impious; and He will change the sun and the moon and the stars. And then He will truly rest on the seventh day. . . .
>
> Furthermore He says to them: "Your new moons and sabbaths I cannot bear with." See how it means: the present sabbaths are not acceptable to me, but what I have made, namely that on which I have given rest to all things and will make beginning of an eighth day, that is the beginning of another world. Wherefore we also celebrate with gladness the eighth day, on which also Jesus rose from the dead and being made manifest ascended into heaven.

Even when we remove the casing of millenarianism—which later Fathers found it easy enough to do if only by an allegorizing method —the primitive celebration of the *mysterion* of redemption remains unimpaired. "On the Lord's day of the Lord, come together, break bread and hold Eucharist. . . ."

> For thine is the power and the glory for ever. Amen.
> Let grace come and let this world pass away!
> Hosanna to the house of David!
> If any man is holy, let him come; if he is not, let him repent!
> *Maranatha!* Amen.[3]

---

[1] Irenaeus *Adv. Haer.* v, 33, 4.
[2] Justin *Dial.* 80.
[3] *Didache*, 14, 1; 10, 5–6.

(C) PASCHA AND PENTECOST

Though St. Paul was unyielding in his principle that Gentile Christians were free from all obligations of the Jewish law, he himself continued to observe the Law in so far as his missionary work allowed him to do so. Thus the "we-source" of Acts presents him hastening to his final rendezvous in Jerusalem so that "if it were possible for him, he would be in Jerusalem for the day of Pentecost" (Acts 20: 16). The same source also notes, at an earlier stage in this last tour of his churches in Greece and Asia Minor, a sailing from Philippi "after the days of Unleavened Bread" (20: 6). St. Paul himself, in 1 Corinthians 16: 8, spoke of remaining in Ephesus "until Pentecost". There is no suggestion or hint in these passages that the feasts were thought of as specifically Christian, rather than Jewish, observances.

Yet certainly a Christian such as St. Paul had a different perspective upon these Jewish feasts by reason of his faith in Christ. 1 Corinthians has been described as a "Paschal letter, a fact which is made particularly clear in its use of Exodus—Numbers, or, more likely, a 'midrash' upon it".[1] It must have been written in the period between Passover and Pentecost. For it looks forward, as indicated in the citation above, to Pentecost as the nearest significant dating point in the immediate days ahead. And it looks backward, surely, to the Passover festival, in the "Christ our Passover is sacrificed for us; therefore let us keep the feast, not with old leaven nor with the leaven of malice and wickedness, but with unleavened bread of sincerity and truth" (5: 7-8). These words themselves are testimony to the Christian transformation of meaning of the old rite. It is not fanciful, therefore, to see in his appeal to the examples (τυπικῶς) of Israel in the wilderness, as warnings to Christians "upon whom the ends of the ages have come", reflections upon the Old Testament lections appointed for the season in the synagogue. And these types drawn from the Exodus experience of the people of the old covenant—such as the water from the rock and the heavenly manna—lead him into discussion of the Church's sacraments of Baptism and Eucharist (see 1 Cor. 10). Is it too early to suppose a special connection of these sacramental observances with the Passover-Pentecost season, as will certainly be the case in a later generation? Perhaps so.

We must return once more, however, to the opening chapters of Acts. The Evangelist dated the beginning of the Church's evangelistic mission and the first baptisms on the Pentecost festival following the

---

[1] P. Carrington, *The Primitive Christian Calendar*, 1952, p. 42.

death and resurrection of Jesus at the preceding Passover. The question is immediately posed as to whether this datum is authentic record of an historical event, or a symbolic introduction to the history of the Church's mission to all peoples that was congenial to the outlook of the Evangelist. Caution in this matter is not due solely to the fact that the Fourth Evangelist preserves a different tradition (John 20: 22): namely, that the Lord imparted the Spirit to His disciples on the day of resurrection itself. Nor is it a matter of the hesitancy of many interpreters about the Evangelist's apparent misunderstanding of the phenomenon of speaking in tongues as though it were a capacity to preach in many languages. The difficulty is a more subtle one and has to do with the structure and purpose of the Evangelist's account of Christian beginnings.

It is a well-known characteristic of the Evangelist's literary method that he generally follows the order of contents of his sources, but freely rewrites his material to conform to his own vocabulary and style.[1] In construction of his two-volume account of Christian origins, he has not only bound them together in a unifying thesis—the universality of God's redeeming purpose in Christ—but he has exhibited real skill in organizing his materials so as to bring this thesis effectively to the conviction of his readers.

Each volume has an introduction which sets the stage for the principal figures of his story, and an initial incident that sums up the outreach of their respective ministries. In the gospel, the introduction embraces chapters 1–3, recording the birth, upbringing, baptism, and genealogy of Jesus.[2] With chapter 4 we are given the two stories of the Temptation and the inauguration of Jesus' public ministry in the synagogue at Nazareth. These initial acts of the Messiah show Him now fully endowed at His baptism with the Holy Spirit (cf. 3: 22; 4: 1) and launched upon His career in the Spirit's power (4: 14). But the Evangelist has deliberately moved the account of Jesus' visit to the Nazareth synagogue to this place, changing the position which it has in his Markan source.[3] And he has further developed the story by an exegesis

[1] See my remarks in *Munera Studiosa*, ed. by M. H. Shepherd, Jr., and S. E. Johnson, 1946, p. 92 and note.

[2] It may seem that only chapters 1–2 belong to this introduction, in view of the formal chronological note that marks the opening of chapter 3. But the first two chapters are in a sense a prologue that has possibly been added at a later stage of development of the gospel.

[3] This is clear from the remark of the people in verse 23, which implies that Jesus had already been at work in Capernaum. The Evangelist has prepared for this only by the summary statement (quite characteristic of his style) in 4: 14–15.

of Isaiah 61: 1-2 placed upon Jesus' lips. The appearance of Jesus at His home-synagogue affords an appropriate occasion for a formal promulgation of His destiny to fulfil the promises of God by His mission to the people of God.

Similarly, the second volume has an introduction, recounting the promise by Jesus of the gift of the Spirit, the ascension, and the filling up of the number of the Twelve by the selection of Matthias. Then in chapter 2 the story of how the gospel was proclaimed to all peoples by the power of the Holy Spirit is inaugurated with the Pentecost experience, the preaching of Peter, and the first baptisms. As we have no source for the Acts volume comparable to the Gospel of Mark, we cannot say categorically that the Evangelist has altered the order of his sources in the interest of a specific thematic construction. But there are hints that the arrangement of material is not in the original form in which it came to him.

For one thing, there are indications in chapters 1-5 of duplicating material, which may or may not be the result of combining two different sources.[1] If so, chapter 2: 1-40 (minus Peter's speech) would be a doublet of 4: 23-31, as the summary in 2: 41-7 appears to be more certainly a doublet of 4: 33-5. If this analysis be correct, the launching of the Church's evangelistic preaching would have had a less grandiose setting than the Pentecost miracle of languages. It would begin with the healing of the lame man at the gate of the Temple, the consequent arrest of the apostles for an unauthorized use of the Name of Jesus, and their valiant defense before the Sanhedrin.[2] In such concrete situations of witness the promise of the Spirit given by the Lord to His disciples was realized (cf. Matt. 10: 19-20; Luke 12: 11-12; John 14: 26, 15: 26—16: 4).

Another indication of displacement of the Pentecost story is provided by the textual variant of 2: 14. The received text reads: "Peter with the eleven", where the Greek idiom means "Peter with the eleven, including himself", not "Peter with the eleven others". Codex Bezae makes a correction in the interest of clarity, and reads: "Peter with the ten apostles." We are thus led to conclude that the story in its original form

---

[1] A. Harnack, *Die Apostelgeschichte*, 1908, pp. 142 ff., identifies a source A (3: 1-5: 16) and a source B (2; 5: 17-42). See *Munera Studiosa*, pp. 100-1.

[2] The arrest for the use of the Name (which is clear from 4: 7) was, according to the author, motivated by a distaste of the Temple authorities for their teaching the people and proclaiming the resurrection. So 4: 2. This may be true, but the Evangelist is obviously more interested in the general motive than the technical charge, and so he colors his narrative accordingly.

either preceded the account of the choice of Matthias, or came from a tradition independent of any story about Matthias. In either case, the Evangelist appears to have utilized the Pentecost story for a purpose other than that of strict chronology.

What that purpose was is not far to seek. The Pentecost story provided the perfect setting for the relation of how the gospel, preached by Spirit-endowed apostles, spread to all the world, to Gentile as well as to Jew. In late Jewish tradition, though not in the Old Testament, Pentecost was associated with the historical memory of the giving of the Law. The Evangelist's account exhibits clear reminiscences of the theophany on Mount Sinai. The comparison is all the more striking if one places the story alongside of Philo's description of this theophany in his work *On the Decalogue* (ix, xi):

I should suppose that God wrought on this occasion a miracle of a truly holy kind by bidding an invisible sound to be created in the air more marvellous than all instruments and fitted with perfect harmonies, not soulless, nor yet composed of body and soul like a living creature, but a rational soul full of clearness and distinctness, which giving shape and tension to the air and changing it to flaming fire, sounded forth like the breath through a trumpet an articulate voice so loud that it appeared to be equally audible to the farthest as well as the nearest. . . .

It was natural that the place should be the scene of all that was wonderful, claps of thunder louder than the ears could hold, flashes of lightning surpassing brightness, the sound of an invisible trumpet reaching to the greatest distance, the descent of a cloud which like a pillar stood with its foot planted on the earth, while the rest of its body extended to the height of the upper air, the rush of heaven-sent fire which shrouded all around in dense smoke. For when the power of God arrives, needs must be that no part of the world should remain inactive, but all move together to do Him service.[1]

To the Evangelist, the outpouring of the Spirit on Pentecost marked the beginning of the new dispensation of God, the new age of the Holy Spirit that replaced the old age of the Law. But there was also in his mind the ancient tale of the Tower of Babel. As God had confounded the schemes of sinful men and separated them by the diversity of languages, now in a new unity of the Spirit all men could be drawn together and reconciled in the gospel of God's marvellous acts, now preached to them irrespective of race or tongue.

The question therefore arises whether the Pentecost story in Acts 2

[1] Translation by F. H. Colson in the Loeb Classical Library edition of Philo, Vol. VII, pp. 23, 29.

reflects a celebration of the festival already established in the Church or is itself the basis upon which the Church at some later time instituted the festival. No certain answer can be given to this question. But there is a datum in the textual tradition of 2: 1 that is not without importance for our inquiry. Foakes Jackson and Lake in their exhaustive commentary on Acts point out the difficulty of translating this verse literally: "at the completion of the day of Pentecost", for verse 15 speaks of the day as only beginning. They are therefore led to believe that the Evangelist intended his Greek construction to mean "towards the completion of the Weeks" that led up to the day of Pentecost.[1] The reading of Codex Bezae makes this more evident: "in those days of the completion of the day of Pentecost." But the Latin and Syriac Peshitto versions refer to the "days of Pentecost", *i.e.*, the season of seven weeks from Passover to Pentecost.

Doubtless the "western" readings of Codex Bezae and the versions reflect the established custom in the Church of celebrating the "great fifty days" from Passover to Pentecost as a Christian festival of the redeeming work of Christ. But this "western" text can be established as having been in existence in the early part of the second century.[2] Irrespective therefore of what the Evangelist himself might have known or intended to express about such a festival, the textual evidence shows us that such a celebration existed in the Church in the post-apostolic age at the latest and before the crisis created by the rise of Gnosticism. The Paschal-Pentecost feast of fifty days might therefore claim with some justification, as Tertullian and Hippolytus in the early third century did claim for it, a basis in apostolic tradition.

[1] See note in *BC* IV, 16–17; cf. Ropes, *ibid.*, III, 10–11.
[2] J. H. Ropes in *BC* III, ccxxiii–iv, ccxl–vi.

II

THE GOSPELS AND THE PASCHA

A NOTABLE trend in recent New Testament study is the increasing interest in the liturgical backgrounds and structures that possibly lie behind the several gospels and epistles. The hypotheses offered to date have not won wide acceptance, although there is a consensus that further pursuit of such investigations may shed new light both upon the origins of much of the New Testament and upon the primitive stages of the Church's worship in the process of its transformation of inherited cultic patterns and materials from Judaism.

For example, Professor G. D. Kilpatrick presented the thesis that the Gospel of Matthew was primarily composed for public reading in the liturgy, though he refrained from any attempt to set out its lectionary scheme in detail.[1] A bolder approach along similar lines has been made for the Gospel of Mark by Archbishop Philip Carrington,[2] who has analysed the gospel pericopes according to a Galilean calendar of Jewish festivals and Sabbaths. A generation ago, Professor B. W. Bacon called attention to the reflection of Roman liturgical usages in the Gospel of Mark, especially in the Passion narrative.[3] Of this we shall have more to say presently. No one has yet made a serious effort to study Luke from this perspective; but the concern of the Fourth Evangelist with the sacraments has been a constant debating ground amongst commentators

[1] *The Origins of the Gospel According to Matthew*, 1946, pp. 72–100.

[2] *The Primitive Christian Calendar*, I, 1952. His thesis has been reviewed negatively by R. P. Casey, "St. Mark's Gospel", *Theology* LV, 1952, pp. 362–70; and by W. D. Davies, "Reflections on Archbishop Carrington's 'The Primitive Christian Calendar' ", *The Background of the New Testament and Its Eschatology*, ed. by W. D. Davies and D. Daube in Honour of Charles Harold Dodd, 1956, pp. 124–52. See the more favorable review of S. E. Johnson, "A New Theory of St. Mark", *ATR* XXXV, 1953, pp. 41–4. Carrington has defended his position in "The Calendrical Hypothesis of the Origin of Mark", *Expository Times* LXVII, 1956, pp. 100–3.

[3] *The Beginnings of Gospel Story* (The Modern Commentary), 1909, pp. 197–8 and *passim*; *Is Mark a Roman Gospel?* (Harvard Theological Studies, VII), 1919; *The Gospel of Mark: Its Composition and Date*, 1925, pp. 172–6.

on the Johannine literature. Dr. Oscar Cullmann's monograph on the subject is the latest and most complete defense of the underlying sacramental interest of the Gospel of John.[1] And one may note in passing recent theories that the Gospel of John is either itself a liturgy, or that its discourses are either hymnodic or homiletic materials for use in the celebration of festivals of the Jewish-Christian Year.[2]

Similarly, in the study of the New Testament epistles, a notable contribution in liturgical interpretation has been Professor F. L. Cross's hypothesis that I Peter is a Paschal liturgy,[3] a thesis that goes well beyond the widespread view that this epistle contains materials from a baptismal homily.[4] Carrington, in his work already cited, has called attention to the midrash on Exodus-Numbers in the Corinthian epistles. I Corinthians, he says, is a Paschal letter; 2 Corinthians is a Pentecostal letter. Their themes derive in part from the synagogue lectionary known to Paul, which was in use during the period from Passover to Pentecost, when these letters were penned. He suggested also that the Epistle to the Hebrews might possibly be a Christian *megillah* for the Day of Atonement.[5]

It is not our purpose here either to re-state or to argue these theories, but to turn our attention to the gospel records, especially that of St. Mark, for whatever light they may throw upon the developing Paschal celebration of the Church in the post-apostolic age. To do this, we must make what may seem at first glance to be an extensive excursus into certain byways of literary criticism, particularly as regards the Passion narrative. In any case, one cannot consider the origins and development of the Paschal celebration of the ancient Church without taking some

[1] *Early Christian Worship* (Studies in Biblical Theology No. 10), 1953, pp. 37–119, a translation of the 2nd edition of *Urchristentum und Gottesdienst*, 1950, with supplement from the French version.

[2] *Ibid.*, p. 59, n. 2, where Cullmann refers to a work I have not seen by W. H. Raney, *The Relation of the Fourth Gospel to the Christian Cultus*, 1933. See also B. W. Bacon, *The Gospel of the Hellenists*, 1933, pp. 138–9; F. C. Grant, *The Gospel of John*, 1956, I, p. 17; F. A. Schilling, "The Liturgy of St. John", *The Living Church* CXXVII, Nov. 29, 1953, pp. 18–19, 29–31 (who refers for his views to A. Greiff, *Das älteste Pascharitual der Kirche*, 1929).

[3] *I Peter, A Paschal Liturgy*, 1954.

[4] R. Perdelwitz, *Die Mysterienreligion und das Problem des I. Petrusbriefes*, 1911; W. Bornemann, "Der erste Petrusbrief—eine Taufrede des Silvanus?" *ZNTW* XIX, 1919–20, pp. 143–65; F. W. Beare, *The First Epistle of Peter*, 1947, pp. 6–9; E. G. Selwyn, *The First Epistle of St. Peter*, 1947, pp. 268–77 (hymns in I Peter), and pp. 305–11 (critique of Perdelwitz's theories).

[5] *Op. cit.*, pp. 42–4.

stand in the seemingly endless controversy over the dating of events that marked the ending of the Lord's earthly life.

(A) THE PASSION NARRATIVE OF MARK

Both the proponents of form-criticism and the advocates of documentary source-criticism agree that the Second Gospel is a reworking of earlier traditions, oral and written, that the Evangelist arranged and interpreted for his own special purposes. The critics may differ respecting the nature and extent of these sources; but most of them agree that the Passion narrative is one of the earliest pieces of the tradition that Mark used and supplemented. But the Passion narrative itself is a skilful fusion of at least two, and possibly more, strands of tradition. If we take it in its most restricted limits—chapters 14–15—and compare it with the Passion narratives of the other gospels, as well as with the summary traditions preserved in the letters of St. Paul and the Book of Acts, we can remove from the Markan narrative at once certain details that are peculiarly Markan and secondary. These include the three-hour datings, the flight of the young man at the arrest of Jesus, the promise of the resurrection in Galilee, the "father of Alexander and Rufus", and so forth. These minor details do not concern us here. More significant are the paragraphs that seem to be expansions awkwardly inserted into what is otherwise a smooth-flowing narrative. These include:

The Anointing at Bethany	14: 3–9
The Preparation for the Supper	14: 12–16
The Agony in Gethsemane	14: 32–42
The Trial before the Sanhedrin	14: 55–65
The Women at the Cross	15: 40–1

Apart from the internal evidence of the Markan Passion narrative itself, the excision of these sections listed can be in some measure supported by the evidence of the Johannine Passion narrative, and to a lesser degree by the evidence from Paul and Acts. The Johannine narrative, which in so much of its ordering and detail conforms to the traditional structure of the Synoptic narratives, places the Anointing before the Entry into Jerusalem, omits the Preparation for the Supper and the Gethsemane scene, makes the session of the Sanhedrin an examination rather than a trial, and employs the tradition of the Women at the Cross for a quite different purpose and reason. If we combine the notices of Paul and Acts about the Passion we get the following incidents:

	Acts	Paul
The Betrayal		1 Cor. 11: 23
The Supper		1 Cor. 11: 24 ff.
The Delivery of Jesus by the	2: 23; 3: 13; 4: 27;	
Jews to Pilate	7: 52; 13: 28	
Barabbas	3: 14	
Crucifixion	10: 39	1 Cor. 15: 3 etc.
Burial	13: 29	1 Cor. 15: 4

For our immediate purpose, we are not so much concerned with the larger problem of the original form of the narrative, as with the two Markan insertions at its beginning: the Anointing at Bethany and the Preparation for the Supper. Almost all critics who give any favor to the subject of "sources" of the Passion narrative view the pericope of the Anointing as an independent unit that Mark has fused into the narrative.[1] It can be dropped out of the story without any disruption of the sense; in fact, the narrative reads more smoothly and logically if one passes directly from 14: 2 to 14: 10. This is not to deny that a tradition of the Anointing belongs with the Passion material from a very early time—the evidence of John supports this. The main question is whether the pericope belongs originally to the place where Mark has put it.

The paragraph recounting the Preparation for the Supper can also be removed without any disruption of the sense; though obviously such a narrative, if it is original at all, belongs in this place. It has been noted that the time allowed for the preparation was unduly short, if Jesus sent the two disciples to make ready the supper only in the morning of the day of the supper itself. Comment has also been made about the fact that once the two disciples were dispatched, there is no statement of their return to Jesus so that they were with the group of twelve that came with Him in the evening to the supper room. These two observations need not carry much weight. The story implies that Jesus had Himself made some preliminary preparations unknown to the disciples. And a day was sufficient time to prepare for a small dinner party. If the supper was a Passover, the two disciples could not in any case have prepared the lamb before the afternoon, when the Paschal lambs were slaughtered in the Temple. The brevity of the narrative should not be

---

[1] F. C. Grant, *The Interpreter's Bible* VII, 866, and V. Taylor, *The Gospel According to St. Mark*, 1952, pp. 524 ff., survey the views of critics from Wellhausen onwards. Both Grant and Taylor agree that the Anointing pericope is secondary (though not necessarily inauthentic)—a significant consensus between a leading advocate of form-criticism and one of the sharpest critics of the limitations of form-criticism.

unduly pressed, to demand some accounting of the successive movements of the two disciples. They might have joined the others at the room rather than have returned to Jesus.

What makes the paragraph appear to be a Markan insertion is the close parallel it forms with the Preparation for the Triumphal Entry (11: 1 ff.).[1] From a literary standpoint, it has the marks of a Markan composition. A point to note especially is the use in this pericope of the term "disciples" instead of the "Twelve". The same word "disciples" occurs also in the Anointing episode and once in the Gethsemane paragraph (14: 32)—both passages, as we have noted, being suspected by many critics of being secondary.[2] Even Dr. Jeremias, who has argued valiantly for the Passover intepretation of the Last Supper, believes that Mark 14: 12–16 comes from "a different cycle of tradition" from that of 14: 1–2, 17 ff.[3] Yet, if verses 12–16 are not an original part of the Passion narrative as it came to Mark—or if they are independent of the source that underlies Mark's material—then the case for the Last Supper being a Passover meal is very materially weakened. For it is exactly verses 12–16 that identify the supper with the Passover meal. Without them, there is no necessity of interpreting the Last Supper in this way.

The removal of verses 12–16 also does away with the problem of Mark's dating in verse 12: "on the first day of unleavened bread, when they sacrificed the Passover." Jeremias has examined thoroughly the inherent contradiction of this dating. He has shown that it is characteristic of Mark's style that, whenever two dates are placed side by side, it is the second one that interprets the first. He believes that the problem is the result of Mark's "faulty translation". But it might be due to his ignorance.[4]

If we are right in removing the pericopes of the Anointing and the Preparation for the Supper from the basic narrative underlying the Markan Passion narrative, we are brought to a tradition that agrees with the Johannine chronology: the Last Supper occurred on the evening of Nisan 14, not the evening of Nisan 15—hence it was not the

---

[1] The material is conveniently laid out in detail by V. Taylor, *op. cit.*, pp. 535–6.
[2] See the Appended Note to this chapter.
[3] J. Jeremias, *The Eucharistic Words of Jesus*, 1955, p. 65.
[4] *Ibid.*, pp. 2–4. One should note the discussion of R. H. Lightfoot, *History and Interpretation in the Gospels*, 1935, pp. 130 ff., who emphasizes the point that the Preparation pericope is the only place that identifies the Last Supper with the Passover. Lightfoot does not take sides, however, on the issue whether the Last Supper was a Passover or not, but affirms that the Preparation pericope has a quite different origin from that of the narrative of the Supper.

Passover. This agreement of Mark's source with the Fourth Gospel was long ago defended ably by B. W. Bacon,[1] and adds force to the position of those scholars who have preferred the Johannine dating (so fully in accord as it is with all that we can deduce from St. Paul), despite the able and acute attack upon it by Jeremias. One has only to read this basic narrative underlying Mark 14: 1 ff. to see this agreement of the Markan source with John:

> It was now two days before the Passover and the feast of Unleavened Bread (*i.e.*, Wednesday, by Mark's chronology), and the chief priests and scribes were seeking how to arrest him by stealth and kill him. For they said, "Not on the feast, lest there be a tumult of the people."

> And Judas Iscariot, one of the Twelve, went to the chief priests in order to betray him to them. And when they heard it they were glad and promised to give him money. And he sought a favorable opportunity to betray him.

> And when it was evening (*i.e.*, either Wednesday or the next day) he came with the Twelve. And as they were reclining and eating, Jesus said, etc.

Mark specifically states that the Crucifixion took place on a Friday (15: 42): "the Preparation, which is the day before the Sabbath." The same dating is given in John 19: 31, except that John makes clear that the Sabbath on this occasion was also the Passover. Mark, however, by his development of the narrative, has made Friday and not the Sabbath the feast of the Passover. It is strange therefore that in speaking of Friday he called it the Preparation (*i.e.*, the day before the Sabbath) and not Passover itself. Possibly we have here another indication of the more primitive tradition underlying Mark, which in this instance the Evangelist has left unaltered and without reinterpretation.

With this reconstruction of the tradition "before Mark", we find that Mark's chronology of "Holy Week" is also the same as John's. The Betrayal probably took place on the morning of the day of the Supper, Thursday. John does not say this explicitly, but implies it in 13: 2. Working backward from the pivotal day Friday, we have the following day by day sequence in Mark:

Friday	Crucifixion
Thursday	Betrayal and Last Supper
Wednesday	Discourses and Controversies
Tuesday	Cursing of Fig Tree and Cleansing of Temple
Monday	Triumphal Entry

[1] See above, p. 27, note 3.

The Gospel of John likewise dates the Entry on Monday (cf. 12: 1, 12). The difference is that John placed the Anointing on Sunday, whereas Mark inserted it on the day of the Betrayal; and, of course, the Fourth Evangelist did not place the Cleansing of the Temple in relation to the Passion narrative. But the broad chronology in Mark's basic source and in John is the same.[1]

In all fairness, it must be stated that the traditions with which Mark supplemented his basic narrative of the Passion—so as to make the Last Supper a Passover—may have been just as primitive and just as "authentic". The debate among scholars regarding the chronology of the Passion may never be resolved, without the discovery of new documents and evidence beyond what we have in the gospels. The valiant effort of Jeremias to uphold the Synoptic sequence and interpretation has won over many waverers. But he has by no means proved his case. He admits that the astronomical calculations of modern scientists are inconclusive. If he attacks the Fourth Evangelist for altering the chronology to suit a theological position, he cannot fairly exonerate Mark from the same *Tendenz*. All recent studies of the Second Gospel emphasize the theological influences at play in Mark's account no less than in John's. The only way still open to resolve the contradiction between the Synoptics and John is that of internal criticism of the narratives themselves. For Mark has "interpreted" the tradition quite as much as the Fourth Evangelist.

The really strong point in Jeremias's favor is the independent witness of Luke 22: 15 to a Passover interpretation of the Last Supper, for this passage of Luke is not dependent upon Mark. But the great defect of Jeremias's able study is the way he overlooks the significance of the secondary character of Mark 14: 12–16, the pericope of the Preparation; and this is the more extraordinary since Jeremias himself admits its secondary character. With this admission, his whole argument is seri-

•

[1] The attempt of A. Jaubert, *La date de la Cène, Calendrier biblique et liturgie chrétienne*, 1957, to establish Tuesday as the day of the Last Supper, on the basis of the calendar of the Book of Jubilees supposedly used by the Qumran community, strikes me as totally unconvincing. (1) It exaggerates the influence of the Qumran Covenanters upon the formation of Christianity. It is the kind of hypothesis one must expect from the enthusiasm engendered by the rich discoveries of the Dead Sea manuscripts. (2) The sole patristic evidence cited by her in confirmation of her thesis consists of the third-century Syrian *Didascalia*, and the fourth-century (and most untrustworthy) Epiphanius. These are entirely too slender props to counterbalance the unanimous witness of the gospels, and the accepted traditions of both Eastern and Western Churches so far as their liturgical usages known.

ously undermined. And the Passover theory of the Last Supper demands, as Vincent Taylor has pointed out, "a remarkable collection of things to be explained".[1]

We are therefore inclined to accept the Johannine chronology as the more plausible. With it, the witness of St. Paul agrees; at the least, it suggests nothing that would contradict it. But there are two other factors that should carry more weight than Jeremias gives them. One is that the Eucharist of the early Church was not viewed as a Christian transformation of the Passover, with the single exception of the Synoptics' interpretation. Not Paul, nor Acts, nor the Apostolic Fathers, nor later writers describe the Eucharist as a "Christian Passover". The word *Pascha* in the Fathers describes the annual celebration of what we call Easter, with its preceding fast. Secondly, despite Jeremias's argument that the word for bread in the gospel accounts of the Last Supper may mean "unleavened bread", there is not the slightest trace in the writings of the early Fathers that the Eucharist was ever celebrated with unleavened bread. The unanimous usage of the Eastern Churches to this day is the employment of leavened bread in the Eucharist; and there is no reference to the use of unleavened bread in the Eucharist of the Western Church before the time of Bede.[2]

(B) THE PASCHA IN THE GOSPEL OF MARK

The Gospel of Mark provides us with the first clear indications of a Christian festival of the Pascha. Written at Rome towards the close of the apostolic period, the Second Gospel, though largely based on Palestinian traditions, was written for Gentile readers with a definite bias against Judaizing. It cannot be proved that the author was even a Jew by birth and upbringing.[3] At no place does he display his antagonism to Judaism in greater degree than in matters of the ceremonial law. It may be that this bias explains why he omits from his account of the Last Supper, which he interprets as a Passover, any command of Jesus to repeat the rite. Surely it is not because Mark opposed the observance of the Eucharist. It may be that he wanted nothing in the way of observance of the Jewish Passover.

Nonetheless, when the Evangelist wrote his gospel, there was already established at Rome a liturgical celebration of the Pascha. This is suggested by the peculiar indications of time sequence in the Markan

[1] *Op. cit.*, p. 667.
[2] Cf. E. Herman, "Azymes", *Dictionnaire de droit canonique*, I, 1584-9.
[3] See the excellent discussion of F. C. Grant, *The Earliest Gospel*, 1943, ch. x.

Passion narrative: (1) the four watches of the night that are mentioned at the conclusion of the "little apocalypse" in 13: 35, and (2) the three-hour periods noted in the Crucifixion narrative in 15: 25, 33. These time indications of a fourfold-night and a fourfold-day division, so characteristic of Roman custom, are found only in Mark. None of the other Synoptic gospels are so precise; and the Gospel of John places the Crucifixion after the sixth hour (19: 14), not as in Mark at the third hour.

This sequence of Mark suggests an observance of an all-night vigil followed by an all-day watch. This is made more plausible by the note in Mark 2: 20: "The days will come, when the Bridegroom shall be taken away from them; and then, they shall fast *on that day*." The "days to come" are certainly here the days after the earthly life of Jesus, and "that day" is the day of the fast before the Christian Pascha. The verse does not refer to the historical Passion of Christ, but to the liturgical Pascha of the Church.[1] It is this very verse to which Tertullian later appealed for the origin of the Church's custom.[2]

One other facet of Mark's narrative calls for comment. Mark always speaks of the resurrection as taking place "after three days" (as in the three predictions of the Passion—8: 31, 9: 31, 10: 34), or "in three days" (as in 14: 58, 15: 29, the latter being the saying about the destruction and rebuilding of the Temple). Mark never uses the locution favored by St. Paul and Luke-Acts, "on the third day". Matthew, in the three Passion predictions, substitutes "on the third day" for "after three days". Yet Matthew preserves, in traditions peculiar to his gospel, relics of the dating "after three days": in the request of the priests and Pharisees to Pilate for a guard at the tomb (27: 64), and more strikingly in the "three days and three nights" typified by Jonah (12: 40). In addition, one should note that the Fourth Gospel like Mark never uses "the third day" of the resurrection, but reflects the Markan usage "in three days" in the saying about the Temple (John 2: 19-20).

Commentators generally gloss over the difference in these two phrases about the resurrection and maintain that they mean the same thing. Undoubtedly the early Christians understood them as synonymous. But they are not necessarily so when taken literally. Long ago, Professor B. W. Bacon called attention to this variation of dating in the tradition.[3] He remarked that the phrase "the third day" was a reflection

---

[1] This interpretation has been held by many commentators since Wellhausen. V. Taylor, *op. cit.*, pp. 211–12, rejects it, however.

[2] *De ieiunio 2.*

[3] *The Beginnings of Gospel Story*, p. 230.

of the Church's Sunday Eucharist, and rested upon the tradition of finding the tomb empty on Sunday morning, presupposing therefore that the Lord had already risen from the dead. Or it may have been due to the "Pauline equivalence" of the risen Christ with the first-fruits. The phrase "after three days", he believed, went back to the primitive tradition of the time of Christ's appearance to the Twelve, which may not have taken place on Sunday.

The lack in Mark of a resurrection-appearance narrative makes it impossible for us to be precise in this question. There is nothing in Mark that indicates specifically that the Christian Pascha must be observed on Sunday other than the finding of the Empty Tomb on the first day of the week. Professor Bacon was probably right in maintaining that Mark was not an innovator in this matter, but merely reflected a custom of a Sunday-Pascha already established.[1] As we have noted, the omission of a command to repeat the Supper may very well fit in with a prejudice against the conformation of the Church's Pascha to the Jewish Passover. The fact remains, however, that Mark with his one-day fast, his vigil and watch, might be reconciled with either a Jewish-Christian observance of the Pascha on any day of the week, or with a Gentile-Christian observance of the Pascha only on Sundays. The point is worth noting here by way of anticipation of our ensuing discussion concerning the controversy over the date of the Pascha in the second century.[2]

The real problem in Mark remains—not the question whether he preferred to observe the Christian Pascha only on Sundays, but why he changed the tradition about the death of Jesus on Nisan 14 to a dating on Nisan 15. As we have said before, there is no definitive solution to this question. For one thing, the alteration may be simply due to Mark's ignorance of Jewish custom (of which there is not a little evidence in his gospel). Or it may be a confusion of a Gentile writer, who counted the day in the Roman manner, with sources that assumed the Jewish reckoning of the day from sunset to sunset. That is, if his Aramaic sources indicated that Nisan 15 began with sundown on Friday, the Evangelist in his simplicity may have understood that all day Friday was to be taken as Nisan 15. It is possible, too, that Mark believed he was being faithful to the Pauline theology, by taking "Christ our Passover" as a reference to the feast itself, and not to the lamb slain on the day of Preparation.

Another possibility, one that we do not recall having encountered in

[1] *Ibid.*
[2] See below, Chapter III.

the voluminous literature on the date of the Passion, is that the contra-diction in dating may go back to the very beginning of the Christian movement because of differing calendars in use among Palestinian and Dispersion Jews. In Palestine and its immediate neighbourhood, the date of the Passover was determined by observation of the phases of the moon. But in the Dispersion, the Jews, as we know from Philo and Josephus, followed a fixed calendar.[1] It is quite possible that in the year Jesus was crucified, the Palestinians observed Passover on Saturday, whereas the Jews of the Dispersion celebrated it on Friday. When the time came to write down the tradition, a Christian living in the Dis-persion, whether he were a Jew or a Gentile convert to the faith, would recall that in the year Jesus died the Passover was observed on Friday. The Fourth Evangelist, with his superior knowledge of Judaism, of Palestine, and of Palestinian traditions, kept unaltered the true and original chronology. This Palestinian remembrance remained longer as "apostolic tradition" in the churches of Asia Minor, where there is enough evidence to show that the Church was more strongly influenced by Judaism and more closely intimate with Palestinian Christians for a longer time than was the case in other provinces.[2] Hence the conditions were to hand for the great controversy over the proper time of obser-vance of the Pascha.

APPENDED NOTE

The Twelve in the Markan Passion Narrative

The traditions about the Twelve belong to the oldest strata of the New Testament sources, but at an early stage they became confused with other interests. In the gospels, the Twelve are constantly merged with a wider group of "disciples", so that it is not always clear whether the term "disciples" refers to the Twelve specifically or to a less precisely defined group. In the Book of Acts and documents of a later generation, the Twelve are time and again con-fused with the "apostles". But St. Paul's letters, which mention the twelve as such only once (1 Cor. 15: 5), show that the term "apostle" was applied to a number of early leaders who were not members of the Twelve. And Acts betrays the same distinction in 14: 4, 14, where Paul and Barnabas are called "apostles", though otherwise the Third Evangelist tends to make the Twelve and the apostles synonymous. The confusion of later tradition begins to become apparent in the resurrection narratives.

[1] Philo *De spec. leg.* ii, 28; Josephus *Ant.* iii, 10, 5.
[2] See below, Chapter III.

37

For the pre-resurrection time, the period of Jesus' earthly life, all that we know about the Twelve and their place in Jesus' mission and purpose is derived from the Gospel of Mark (with the parallel passages in Matthew and Luke), and one saying preserved in variant form by Matthew and Luke in the material commonly designated as Q. In Luke 22: 29–30, the Q saying about the Twelve is incorporated in a body of teaching about greatness in the kingdom of God that is also known to Mark (10: 28–30). Matthew inserts his form of the Q saying (19: 28–29) in a context featuring Peter and the "disciples" that is also known to Mark (10: 28–30). Thus both Matthew and Luke find a place for the saying in materials that Mark associates with the Twelve: the theme of greatness in the kingdom. It would not be unreasonable to suppose that Mark was himself familiar with the Q saying, but omitted it from his gospel for reasons known only to himself. Be that as it may, with the exception of this one saying, all that we know about the Twelve before the resurrection is ultimately derived from Mark.

We have noted that the oldest strata in Mark's Passion narrative speak of the Twelve; but the pericopes that speak of "disciples" are probably secondary (the Anointing, Preparation of the Supper, Gethsemane, etc.). A closer examination of Mark reveals the fact that the Twelve are seldom mentioned except in contexts that relate to the Passion. The principal exception is the account of the choice and sending forth of the Twelve (3: 13–19 and 6: 7–13). The first of these passages is so obviously out of place that it is impossible to tell exactly where it belongs in the chronology of Jesus' ministry. The pericope begins upon a mountain and ends in a house, and it is set between two pericopes that place Jesus by the seaside. Almost by itself, this pericope of the Selection of the Twelve proves that Mark's order of the ministry of Jesus is his own construction. The pericope of the Sending is less awkwardly introduced into the flow of the narrative, though it could be removed without any loss in the sense. It shows familiarity with the same traditions that underlie the Sending narratives in Matthew and Luke.

After these two instances of the choice and commissioning of the Twelve, Mark does not refer to the number any more until he reaches the third prediction of the Passion (for 4: 10 includes others with the Twelve, and 4: 10–12 are certainly a late insertion into the tradition). Immediately after the third prediction of the Passion, we have the pericope of the Request of James and John, with its reference to the "ten" others, and the words of Jesus about greatness in the kingdom and His own life-giving as a ransom for many. The only other reference to the Twelve comes in the note at 11: 11, that after the Entry and visit to the Temple, Jesus went out to Bethany with the Twelve. Otherwise, the expanded narrative of the Entry, the Cursing of the Fig Tree, and the prediction of the Destruction of the Temple, all bring to the fore "disciples". The apocalyptic discourse of chapter 13, however, is delivered to three named members of the group of the Twelve.

We would not propose the thesis that Mark had available to him a "source", in the customary sense of that word, that revolved around the Twelve.[1] Yet the juxtaposition of the material in Mark that mentions the Twelve is nonetheless of considerable interest in that it suggests a connection of the Twelve with the basic stratum of Mark's Passion narrative. Except for the expansion of the Sending pericope (6: 7–13), this material holds together with a surprising consistency, and might be placed apart in a separate and coherent narrative by itself:

1. The Choice of the Twelve (with the note in 3: 19a about Judas as the betrayer);
2. The Prediction of the Passion on the way to Jerusalem;
3. The Request of James and John, with the teaching to the Twelve of the true nature of the kingdom that Jesus establishes with His death;
4. The Entry into Jerusalem, and quick retirement with the Twelve to Bethany;
5. The Betrayal;
6. The Last Supper;
7. The Arrest, and subsequent events of the Passion.

If Mark's gospel is incomplete—and there is no necessary reason to consider it as such—its ending would doubtless have contained an Appearance to the Twelve, such as one finds in Matthew 28: 16. The Resurrection Appearance to the Twelve (actually "eleven") in Matthew took place upon a mountain in Galilee. The appointment of the Twelve in Mark 3: 13 also took place upon a mountain in Galilee. Possibly there is a connection between these two incidents; for, as already noted, the Markan pericope is obviously out of place in the context. In the course of oral transmission it would have been quite possible for the account to develop in divergent settings.

Thus the story of the Twelve began with Jesus' selection of them on a mountain in Galilee. It proceeded to relate their going with Him to Jerusalem, in high hopes of His inauguration of the kingdom, only there to end in His betrayal and death, but not before Jesus had given them an explanation of the true nature of His kingdom and of their place in it. Finally, the story concluded with the giving of an earnest of that kingdom in the New Covenant rite of the Last Supper, the Crucifixion, and the appearance of the risen Lord to the Twelve and His commission to them, at the mountain top in Galilee where He had selected them.

We would protest, in any case, against the notion of certain critics that the Twelve as a delimited group of disciples belong merely to a post-Resurrection tradition or constitute an invention of the early Church.[2] Apart from the fact

---

[1] This was the position of Ed. Meyer, *Ursprung und Anfänge des Christentums,* 1921–23, I, 135–47. It has been revived by W. L. Knox, *The Sources of the Synoptic Gospels: I St. Mark,* 1953, pp. 17–31, 115 ff. Cf. the adverse criticism of V. Taylor, *op. cit.,* pp. 74–5.

[2] See the discussion of R. Schütz, *Apostel und Jünger,* 1921, pp. 69–75; and, in rebuttal, the remarks of K. H. Rengstorf in *ThWb* II, 325–6.

that the Twelve may have been the earliest witnesses of the Resurrection and the first leaders and organizers of the Church, the whole history of the apostolic age, in so far as it can be recovered from the New Testament, shows that this particular group had no special role as a group in the ongoing development of the Church. A wider group of apostles took their place at a very early stage, and into this wider group the Twelve were merged and later confused. Only this circumstance explains why the tradition could not remember with exactness the actual names of the Twelve. One cannot harmonize the lists of names in the gospels and in Acts, not to speak of lists in uncanonical sources, without an unwarranted degree of manipulation.[1]

Moreover there is no clear evidence of any motive in the early Church for inventing the Twelve. The obvious suggestion that the Twelve symbolize the twelve tribes of Israel provides a much better motive for their choice by Jesus Himself, than for any invention by a community that so quickly reached out to proselytize the Gentile world. The significance of the Twelve must be sought in the record of the earthly life of Jesus.

[1] See the note of K. Lake in *BC* V, 41–6, and W. H. P. Hatch, "The Apostles in the New Testament and in the Ecclesiastical Tradition of Egypt", *HTR* XXI, 1928, pp. 147–61.

III

THE CONTROVERSY ABOUT THE PASCHA

THE LATTER half of the second century was witness to a controversy in the Church of increasing intensity and bitterness over the proper date for the observance of the Christian Pascha. The chief parties in this debate were the churches of Asia Minor and of Rome. The former group observed the Pascha on the 14th of the Jewish month Nisan, irrespective of what day of the week it fell—hence their name Quartodecimans. The latter, followed by the churches in other provinces of the Roman world, always observed the Pascha on the Sunday following the 14th of Nisan. The meagreness of our sources for this "Quartodeciman" controversy is matched only by the wealth of interpretations of it by modern scholars. The most recent survey of the evidence has produced the theory that the Fourth Evangelist altered the primitive chronology of the Passion of Jesus, and that Quartodeciman practice, based upon this gospel, did not antedate its publication.[1] We would maintain, on the contrary, that Quartodecimanism represents the original practice of the Church, and that the change to a celebration of the Pascha on Sundays was first suggested by the Gospel of Mark. This change became the norm in all churches except those of Asia Minor when the Gospel of Matthew was widely accepted as authoritative.

We have recounted in a previous chapter how the early Jewish Christians continued to observe the round of Sabbaths and festivals prescribed in the Jewish Law, to which they added the new Christian keeping of Sunday as the day for the eucharistic celebration.[2] St. Paul himself was no exception to this custom, even though many Jewish Christians thought him little less than an apostate. But, as we have noted, even though St. Paul observed the Jewish festivals, he was adamant in his insistence that Gentile converts were free from any such

---

[1] A. A. McArthur, *The Evolution of the Christian Year*, 1953, pp. 77–107. See also references in note 2, p. 45 below.

[2] See above, p. 22.

obligation "with regard to a festival or a new moon or a Sabbath" (cf. Col. 2: 16; Gal. 4: 10). Thus the Gentile Christians had no "holy day" other than Sunday.

We have also seen that the Gospel of Mark provides the first notices of an annual Pascha observed at Rome by the Gentile Christians for whom his gospel was written. At the same time the evidence of Mark is ambiguous, because of the way in which his gospel ends, respecting the day of this Paschal celebration, whether it conformed to the Jewish Passover or was always observed on Sunday. The latter seems the more likely. But his narrative could in any case be interpreted in the Jewish way.

The Gospels of Matthew and Luke were published later than Mark— how much later we cannot say precisely, but they were certainly both in circulation by the end of the first century. These gospels were also written for Gentile Christians, and both of them emanate (or at least much of their traditions) from the Gentile churches of Palestine-Phoenicia-Syria.[1] They took over the Markan chronology of the Passion, but corrected the confused dating of Mark 14: 12, and added fuller accounts of the resurrection appearances on the Sunday after the crucifixion. Although both Matthew and Luke contain a generous amount of purely Jewish-Christian tradition, there is no mistaking their basic non-Jewish perspective. These gospels, and the Book of Acts with them, are the charter documents of the Church's universal mission to all peoples among the Gentiles; and both Evangelists reflect in great measure the anti-Jewish temper that seems to have swept through the Church with increasing momentum towards the close of the first and the opening of the second centuries. Their publication appears to have taken place on the eve of those more extreme, heretical movements that began with Docetism and were pursued with vigor in the second century by Marcion and the Gnostics, when the whole Old Testament tradition was attacked as alien to the gospel.

The strongest ties of second generation Gentile Christianity with the old Jewish-Christian traditions of an orthodox character were maintained not in Palestine, but in Asia Minor. One needs only to recall the intimacies there of Papias and Polycarp with disciples of the Lord and with those who knew such disciples. It was in Asia Minor that Philip, one of the Seven, and his prophetess daughters settled; and there gathered the circle of associates of the ever-elusive and mysterious "John". The conflict of Gentile Christians with Judaizing tendencies of

[1] This is generally admitted with regard to Matthew, less commonly so in regard to Luke. See my brief comments in *The Interpreter's Bible*, VII, 217.

one sort or another seems to have persisted longer in Asia Minor. The Fourth Gospel, for all its "Jewishness" of style, knowledge, and content, contains the sharpest polemic of all the gospels against "the Jews". Nonetheless it preserved the original, Palestinian tradition concerning the chronology of the Passion. The strength of Judaizing tendencies in the area is also witnessed by the warnings of the letters of the Apocalypse and of Ignatius. By contrast, Roman documents of the same period, such as 1 Clement and the *Shepherd* of Hermas, appear relatively free of this obsession with Jewish influence.

We cannot determine precisely the time when the majority of the Gentile churches, outside of Asia Minor, adopted the custom of celebrating the Pascha on a Sunday. We suspect, however, that the matter became a cause of controversy mainly through the adoption of Matthew, and with it of the other Synoptic gospels, as authoritative, canonical books. In Palestine and Syria, Matthew quickly became the favored gospel for ecclesiastical discipline and teaching. This is reflected in the Epistle of James, the *Didache*, and the letters of Ignatius.[1]

In the case of the Roman Church, we possess at least a few hints of the development there. Though Eusebius says that the Roman Church and its allies in the controversy with the Quartodecimans followed an "apostolic tradition",[2] the documents he quotes make no such claim. The letter of Irenaeus to Pope Victor specifically says that Pope Anicetus, in his exchange of opinions on the subject with Polycarp, appealed to "the custom of the presbyters before him". Irenaeus himself, in reminding Victor of these presbyters, traces the names only to the time of Pope Sixtus.[3] The pontificate of Sixtus is associated, in a tradition preserved in a fifth-century Syriac document which many scholars consider genuine, with a council at Rome that accepted Matthew as canonical.[4] Professor Bacon hinted that there was possibly a connection between this acceptance at Rome of Matthew's gospel and the establishment of the Sunday Pascha in the Roman Church. The *Liber Pontificalis*, a not very trustworthy source for papal history at so early a period, ascribes the decree of Roman observance of the Pascha on a Sunday to Pope Pius I.[5]

In any event, there is no trace in the fragmentary documents that

[1] See my article, "The Epistle of James and the Gospel of Matthew", *JBL* LXXV, 1956, pp. 40–51.
[2] *H.E.* v, 23, 1.
[3] *Ibid.* v, 24, 14.
[4] See the full discussion in B. W. Bacon, *Studies in Matthew*, 1930, pp. 50–9.
[5] Edited by L. Duchesne, I, 132.

have survived that the Sunday Pascha at Rome was based upon an appeal to Peter or to "apostolic tradition". It is possible, even probable, that Gentile Christians in Rome observed the Sunday Pascha as early as the time of writing of Mark's gospel, or even before. But there is no evidence that this custom became *official* before the first quarter of the second century, at a time when Matthew's gospel was adopted as authoritative.

The acceptance of Matthew in Asia Minor produced controversy among the Quartodecimans themselves. So late as Papias's time—if we may take him as typical of his generation in Asia Minor—oral tradition was preferred to the authority of written gospels. Papias apparently accepted Matthew, with the allowance of some freedom in its interpretation.[1] He had less esteem for Mark. There is nothing in his brief *testimonia* preserved by Eusebius to indicate that he would have permitted either of these gospels to override the living voice of tradition as he had received it in his church. Again, towards the middle of the century, Polycarp and Pope Anicetus in their several positions concerning the celebration of the Pascha both appealed to traditions they had received and not to any written gospel authority. The first intimations that the gospels themselves were a factor in the dispute come from the 160's, through a citation of Eusebius from Melito of Sardis' work on the Pascha.[2] To this dispute belong, no doubt, the obscure fragments preserved in the *Chronicon Paschale* from writings of Claudius Apollinaris, Clement of Alexandria, and Hippolytus. Of these, the fragments of Apollinaris, a successor of Papias in the see of Hierapolis, are the most significant.

The majority of modern scholars have assumed that the dispute over the Pascha in Asia Minor in the 160's was the same as that between Polycarp and Pope Anicetus a decade earlier and between Polycrates of Ephesus and Pope Victor in the 190's, *i.e.*, between Quartodecimans and the advocates of a Sunday Pascha. This interpretation was strongly opposed by Dr. F. E. Brightman,[3] who considered the controversy to be one amongst the Quartodecimans themselves. The problem is further complicated by the different opinions respecting the allegiance of Claudius Apollinaris. Most critics have taken Apollinaris to have been a Quartodeciman. Professor C. C. Richardson, however, insisted that he was not a Quartodeciman—principally on the grounds that Poly-

---

[1] Eusebius *H.E.* iii, 39, 16. Possibly Papias's remark that "each one interpreted them as he was able" included variant positions on the Paschal chronology.
[2] *Ibid.*, iv, 26, 3.
[3] "The Quartodeciman Question", *JTS* XXV, 1924, p. 254.

crates of Ephesus omitted his name from the list of his authorities for Quartodeciman custom.[1]

Whatever may be the truth in these disputed points, the fragments of Apollinaris are not obscure, so far as regards his own views. He did not believe that the Last Supper was a *typikon Pascha*; that is to say, he accepted the Johannine chronology. He was particularly grieved at the ignorance of certain persons who maintained that the Last Supper was a Passover, and who supported their position on the basis of Matthew. In his own exposition of the gospel, Apollinaris used both Matthew and John to set forth the true Pascha of the Lord, "the great sacrifice", as having taken place on the 14th of Nisan and the burial of Christ as having been on the same day. For Apollinaris, the Pascha was not the Supper, but the victory of Christ on the Cross for our redemption.

The most natural reading of these fragments suggests to us that Apollinaris was a Quartodeciman, and that to his basic Johannine chronology he had succeeded in harmonizing Matthew. His interpretation is not basically different from that of Melito of Sardis, if the *Homily on the Passion* recently discovered and edited by Professor Campbell Bonner really is a work of Melito.[2] The fragment from Hippolytus is more obscure, since we do not know the exact personages to whom it refers. It reads:

> I see then that it is a work of strife. For he says thus: "Christ made the Passover then on the day and suffered; therefore it is necessary for me to do also just as the Lord did. For this is the Pascha fore-heralded and completed on the appointed day."

The person quoted by Hippolytus thus took the same position as the opponents of Apollinaris; namely, the Last Supper was a Passover

---

[1] Dr. Richardson's view that the Quartodecimans defended their practice on the basis of the Synoptic chronology does not seem to me convincing. It depends too much on the debatable question of the allegiance of Apollinaris, whom he takes to have been an opponent of Quartodecimanism. See his articles, "The Quartodecimans and the Synoptic Chronology", HTR XXXIII, 1940, pp. 177–90; "Early Patristic Evidences for the Synoptic Chronology of the Passion", ATR XXII, 1940, pp. 299–308. Richardson's view of Apollinaris is shared by J. Quasten, *Patrology*, I, 1950, p. 229. Of course, both sides in the controversy appealed to the gospels, and found their own respective ways of harmonizing them. But note that Polycrates of Ephesus (in Eusebius *H.E.* iv, 24, 3) distinctly appealed to the Fourth Gospel in support of Quartodecimanism.

[2] *Studies and Documents* XII, 1940. The authenticity of this homily has been recently questioned by P. Nautin, *Le dossier d'Hippolyte et de Méliton*, 1953, pp. 46–56.

meal, after which the Lord was crucified. But without the context we cannot tell what relation the person quoted had to the whole dispute. The fragment of Clement of Alexandria is of no help. It reveals only the skill of Clement as a harmonizer of the gospels.

The significance of these fragments lies in their revelation that, once the chronology of the Synoptics was seriously brought to bear upon the Quartodeciman practice, it was shattering to the Asian custom. The Quartodecimans put all their weight into the position that the death of Christ fulfilled the type of the slaughter of the Paschal lamb on the 14th of Nisan, that there was an exact correspondence between the Law and the gospel. The strength of their position so far as their opponents were concerned lay in the fact that it was orthodox. The early writers of the Church, with but rare exceptions, referred the Paschal lamb to Christ as a lamb slain or sacrificed, not a lamb that was eaten. The only passages in the extant writings of the second century that refer the Passover to the Supper and not to the Cross are the two "opponents" of Apollinaris and Hippolytus, respectively, and a single reference in Irenaeus.[1] If the Last Supper was a Passover, as the Synoptics maintained, then the whole rich theology of the Cross as the true Passover for the redemption of mankind was threatened. The Quartodecimans were not interested in a Paschal interpretation of the Eucharist, but of the Cross. In this they were at one with their Sunday-Pascha opponents. As Irenaeus noted, the controversy revolved around the nature of the fast and the dating of the Pascha, not about the character of the Paschal celebration nor its essential meaning. There is no support for the position of certain scholars that the Quartodeciman celebration of the Pascha, other than the date, was ordered in a different way from that of other churches. It consisted of a fast, night-vigil—possibly with baptismal initiation—and concluding Eucharist on the morning of the 14th of Nisan.[2]

The obvious way out of their dilemma was for the Quartodecimans to give up their ancient, apostolic custom and adopt the newer practice of observing the Pascha on a Sunday. For to observe the Pascha on

---

[1] Irenaeus *Adv. Haer.* ii, 22, 3; but in iv, 10, 1, Irenaeus distinctly refers the Pascha to the Cross. For this reason I cannot follow Professor Richardson's attempt (see note 1, p. 45 above) to make the Fathers agree with the Synoptic chronology. Quite the opposite seems to me the case; *e.g.*, see all the references in Justin Martyr to the Pascha: *Dial.* xl, 1–2; xlvi, 2; lxxii, 1; cxi, 35—all of which refer to the lamb *slain*.

[2] So Brightman, *op. cit.*; see also O. Casel, "Art und Sinn der ältesten christlichen Osterfeier", *Jahrbuch für Liturgiewissenschaft* XIV, 1934, pp. 1 ff.; J. Jeremias in *ThWb* V, 900–3.

Sunday had two very distinct advantages: (1) It did not contradict any of the gospels, since all of them maintained that Christ had died on Friday and had risen on Sunday; and (2) there was no longer any possibility of inverting the true order of the Law and the gospel as they had received them—that is, the sacrifice must precede the feast. The true character of the Last Supper on Thursday evening would no longer be momentous in its consequences, whether it were a Passover or not. So long as the Quartodecimans clung to their celebration of the 14th of Nisan as the festival of Redemption, they were in danger of having it undercut by those who insisted that the Lord had already accomplished the Passover the preceding evening.

Our last glimpse of the controversy is the picture of Polycrates of Ephesus and his Asian colleagues stubbornly holding to their tradition. But one senses in his weary reply to Pope Victor the last stand of a lost cause. The future lay with Gentiles, for whom, as Hippolytus said, the Pascha "is understood by faith, not kept strictly in the letter".[1]

---

[1] *Philosophumena* viii, 18. See above, p. 14.

IV

THE CHURCH'S PASCHA c. A.D. 200

THE RECOVERY and identification of the *Apostolic Tradition* of Hippo-lytus of Rome has made it possible to reconstruct with considerable detail the outline and character of the Church's Paschal celebration and ceremonies at the turn of the third century. Though but few fragments of the original Greek text of the work have survived, collation of later versions, both in Latin and in the Oriental languages, provides a reasonably accurate transcript of its contents.[1] In recent years the generally accepted positions of modern scholars concerning the person and work of Hippolytus have been seriously questioned.[2] But to date no significant doubt has been raised respecting the relative date of composition of the *Apostolic Tradition*—i.e., within a few years before or after

---

[1] The identification was made independently by E. Schwartz, *Über die pseudoapostolischen Kirchenordnungen* (Schriften der wissenschaftlichen Gesellschaft in Strassburg, 6), 1910, and by R. H. Connolly, *The So-Called Egyptian Church Order and Derived Documents* (Texts and Studies, VIII, 4), 1916. The most convenient edition, by reason of its apparatus criticus, is that of G. Dix, *The Treatise on the Apostolic Tradition of St. Hippolytus of Rome*, 1937. But Dix's own reconstructions of the text are not always reliable. One should check them by reference to the edition of B. S. Easton, *The Apostolic Tradition of Hippolytus*, 1934.

For the text of the Latin version, one should still refer to its *editio princeps* in E. Hauler, *Didascaliae Apostolorum Fragmenta Veronensia Latina*, 1900. The Coptic, Arabic, and Ethiopic versions may be found in G. Horner, *The Statutes of the Apostles or Canones Ecclesiastici*, 1904. More recently, the Ethiopic text has been published by H. Duensing, *Der äthiopische Text der Kirchenordnung Hippolyts* (Abhandlungen der Akademie der Wissenschaften in Göttingen, Philol.-hist. Klasse, III, 32), 1946, and the Coptic text by W. Till and J. Leipoldt, *Der koptische Text der Kirchenordnung Hippolyts* (Texte und Untersuchungen, 58. Band), 1954.

[2] P. Nautin, *Hippolyte et Josipe*, 1947, and *Le dossier d'Hippolyte et de Méliton*, 1953. For a bibliography of the controversy aroused by M. Nautin's theories, see *Patrologia Orientalis* Tome XXVII, Fasc. 1 and 2, 1954, pp. 271–2; B. Altaner, *Patrologie* (5th ed., 1958), pp. 148–9. See also A. Amore, "Note su S. Ippolito Martire", *Rivista di archeologia cristiana* XXX, 1954, pp. 63–97.

A.D. 200[1]—nor has there been any disposition to contest the fact that its place of origin was the church in Rome.[2]

If we grant that the customs recorded in the *Apostolic Tradition* are a faithful witness to Church practices at Rome about 200, we must still answer the question as to the reliability of the claim that this tradition is apostolic. In the first place, it may be noted that Hippolytus' contemporary in the church at Carthage, Tertullian, testifies to a tradition from apostolic times of almost identical liturgical usages and customs; and this testimony is quite independent of any familiarity by Tertullian with Hippolytus' treatise.[3] Moreover, the work of Tertullian *On Baptism* provides many parallels of detail with at least that portion of Hippolytus' treatise that deals with the Paschal ceremonies.

The general outline of Sunday and Paschal celebrations described by Hippolytus is corroborated a half-century earlier than his time, at Rome, by Justin Martyr.[4] And some of it is suggested as early as A.D. 112 in the province of Bithynia by the famous and much-discussed letter of Pliny the Younger.[5] More significant still is the fact that all of the major elements in Hippolytus' Paschal rite can be supported by evidence from the Pauline epistles or the Book of Acts—the exorcisms, vigil, baptism, laying on of hands with prayer, the kiss of peace, and the eucharistic celebration. Of course, no single passage in the New Testament presents these customs in a single liturgical order specifically related to the Paschal season. But there is nothing in the *ordo* of Hippolytus that could not have been practised in the first century. While we must make allowance for developments and innovations in the second century, especially in view of the crystallizing of hierarchical order and discipline in reaction to the Gnostic crisis, it is reasonable to suppose that patterns of liturgical usage claiming to be apostolic about the year 200 had some basis of fact in the Church's life in the first century.

[1] A strong case for dating the *Apostolic Tradition* in the early years of Pope Zephyrinus, rather than after the break of Hippolytus with Pope Callistus, has been made by C. C. Richardson, "The Date and Setting of the Apostolic Tradition of Hippolytus", *ATR* XXX, 1948, pp. 38–44.

[2] Even P. Nautin affirms the Roman origin of an "*Apostolic Tradition*", which he ascribes to his anti-pope Josephus. See his *Hippolyte contre les hérésies*, 1949, pp. 222, 226–30.

[3] *De corona* 3–4. See J. Quasten, "Tertullian and 'Traditio' ", *Traditio* II, 1944, pp. 481–4.

[4] *Apol.* i, 61; 65–7.

[5] In his baptismal interpretation of Pliny's phrase, *stato die ante lucem*, etc., we are in accord with H. Lietzmann, "Die liturgischen Angaben des Plinius", *Geschichtliche Studien für Albert Hauck zum 70. Geburtstage*, 1916, pp. 34–8.

Be that as it may, another question arises. How far is this liturgy described at Rome typical of other areas of the Church? We have already noted the strong evidence in Tertullian for parallel usages at the time in North Africa. Unfortunately, our sources for the Paschal liturgy in the Eastern churches about 200 are much less extensive. The relevant materials have been collected and commented upon in a survey made by the late Dom Odo Casel.[1] We have the fragments surviving from the Quartodeciman controversy that have already been discussed. There remain also significant traditions from the Paschal homilies delivered by leading churchmen of this age.[2] The scattered references to the Pascha in the extant works of Origen, and notably a surviving letter of his pupil, Bishop Dionysius of Alexandria, to one Basilides, a bishop of the churches in the Pentapolis (Cyrenaica), suggest that the character of the Paschal celebration in Egypt was not materially different from that of Rome.[3] Of especial value is the summary of Paschal customs obtaining in Syria about the middle of the third century, as outlined in the *Didascalia Apostolorum*, an anonymous Church Order that seems not to have been dependent in any way upon the work of Hippolytus.[4]

One may, of course, fill out the picture presented by Hippolytus by reference to the more copious sources of the fourth and fifth centuries, both from the East and the West. This would be methodologically unacceptable were it not for the fact that the pattern of Paschal celebration, even in these later ages, exhibits a fundamental unity of design in

---

[1] "Art und Sinn der ältesten christlichen Osterfeier", *Jahrbuch für Liturgiewissenschaft* XIV, 1934, pp. 1–78.

[2] See C. Bonner, *The Homily on the Passion by Melito Bishop of Sardis with Some Fragments of the Apocryphal Ezekiel* (Studies and Documents XII), 1940. The authenticity of this homily by Melito has been questioned by P. Nautin, *Le dossier d'Hippolyte et de Méliton*, pp. 46–56. We are indebted to P. Nautin, however, for two excellent volumes of *Homélies Pascales* (Sources chrétiennes), 1950, 1953, containing fourth-century Paschal sermons that are based upon earlier homilies by Hippolytus and Origen, respectively.

One should not overlook also the concluding chapters of the *Epistle to Diognetus* xi–xii. In our opinion, these constitute a fragment of a Paschal homily of uncertain authorship. See the recent surveys of H. G. Meecham, *The Epistle to Diognetus*, 1949, pp. 64–8; and H. I. Marrou, *A Diognète* (Sources chrétiennes), 1951, pp. 219 ff.

[3] Dionysius' letter cannot be precisely dated, but it is not likely to be later than 262. See edition by C. L. Feltoe, *The Letters and Other Remains of Dionysius of Alexandria*, 1904, pp. 91–105.

[4] Ch. 21 (ed. R. H. Connolly, 1929, pp. 189–92). Connolly does not believe the evidence strong enough to prove dependence upon Hippolytus—see his introduction, p. lxxxiii.

all the churches. Yet one must exercise caution in using them. The earliest detailed description of the Paschal liturgy in the Eastern sphere dates from the middle of the fourth century and is found in the Catechetical Lectures of Cyril of Jerusalem.[1] It must be remembered always, however, that the liturgical customs of the church in Jerusalem, as they developed in the fourth century, exercised a very great influence upon the rites of all the other churches by reason of its prominence, after Constantine, as a focus of pilgrimage for devout churchmen from every place.

(A) THE FAST

The directives in Hippolytus' *Apostolic Tradition* for the admission and training of candidates for Baptism belong rather to a history of the catechumenate than to a consideration of the Paschal rite itself.[2] At how early a time the churches organized a formal "catechesis" preparatory to their sacramental initiation, one cannot say with certainty. The *Didache* (7: 1) provides evidence of such a custom at a relatively early period.[3] And it is more than likely that catechetical preparation is reflected in the Epistle to the Hebrews:

> Therefore let us leave the elementary teaching about Christ and go on to maturity, not laying again a foundation of repentance from dead works and of faith toward God, with instruction about baptisms and laying on of hands, the resurrection of the dead and eternal judgment. . . . For it is impossible to restore again to repentance those who have once been enlightened, and have tasted of the heavenly gift, and have been made partakers of the Holy Spirit (6: 1–4).

[1] A convenient edition is that of F. L. Cross, *St. Cyril of Jerusalem's Lectures on the Christian Sacraments* (Texts for Students No. 51), 1951.

[2] H. J. Holtzmann, "Die Katechese der alten Kirche", *Theologische Abhandlungen* (Carl von Weizsäcker zu seinem siebzigsten Geburtstage . . .), 1892, pp. 60–110; W. Bousset, *Jüdisch-christlicher Schulbetrieb in Alexandria und Rom* (Forschungen zur Religion und Literatur des Alten und Neuen Testaments 23), 1915; G. Bardy, "L'Église et l'enseignement pendant les trois premiers siècles", *Revue des Sciences religieuses* XII, 1932, pp. 1–28; D. van den Eynde, *Les normes de l'enseignement chrétien dans la littérature patristique des trois premiers siècles*, 1933.

[3] The most recent editor and commentator of the *Didache* rejects as a third-century interpolation the reference in 7, 1 to instruction in the "Two Ways" before Baptism. But his evidence is solely the lack of this phrase in the revision of the *Didache* in *Apostolic Constitutions* vii, 22. This seems to me too slender a support for rejecting the manuscript tradition which we possess in both the Jerusalem MS. and the Georgian version. See J. P. Audet, *La Didaché, Instructions des Apôtres*, 1958, p. 358.

It is easy to surmise why a catechumenate should have developed, at least as early as the close of the apostolic age. Converts were by that time being drawn almost entirely from heathenism, without that background in Judaism such as the Gentile god-fearers had whom we meet in the narrative of Acts. These pagans would require a longer time to be made familiar with the Scriptures and the theological and ethical principles of a faith rooted in the Scriptures. The rise of heresy, first through Docetic tendencies and later in the Gnostic systems, would serve only to increase the need for thorough-going instructions. The threat of persecution, too, would make it necessary for the Church to establish some kind of screening with respect to volunteers for membership; hence the requirement of sponsors to attest the candidates' sincerity and their quality of character that would make them firm in resisting the pressures of opposition.

It was out of the disciplines connected with the catechumenate that the season of Lent was to develop.[1] The fifth canon of the Council of Nicaea in 325 has commonly been taken as the first reference to the "Forty Days" of Lent.[2] But in Hippolytus' directions the period of intensive preparation for candidates specifically chosen for Baptism at the Pascha is not so precisely defined. He simply notes that "from the day they are chosen" the candidates are to receive a daily imposition of hands and exorcism, and are to be admitted at the Eucharist to hear the Gospel lesson.[3] Then on the "fifth day of the week", i.e., on Thursday before the Pascha, the candidates are directed to cleanse themselves by a bath. On Friday and Saturday a strict fast is to be kept, not only by the candidates (xx, 7) but also by all the faithful (xxix, 1). Finally, on Saturday, sometime before the vigil rite begins, the bishop is to give a final screening to the candidates—what later came to be known as a "scrutiny"—by assembling them together for prayer, imposition of hands, exorcism, and the ceremony of breathing on their faces and sealing their foreheads, ears and noses.[4] By these actions the candidates are

---

[1] See the perceptive note of Dix, *op. cit.*, pp. 81-2.

[2] A recent interpretation of the "Forty Days" in the fifth canon of the Council suggests that the term refers not to Lent, but to Ascension Day; see J. G. Davies, *He Ascended Into Heaven*, 1958, pp. 196–8.

[3] The exclusion of catechumens from hearing the Gospel seems to have been a peculiarity of the Roman Church, and the custom survived there at least until the sixth century. See J. A. Jungmann, *The Mass of the Roman Rite*, 1951–55, I, 261, 443. Jungmann, however, seems to imply that the custom only came into use in the revisions of the Roman liturgy in the sixth century.

[4] These ceremonies were undoubtedly created in imitation of the Lord's acts of healing and exorcism as recorded in the gospels, especially Mark 7: 33–5. In later

"purified"—freed from all evil and demonic influences—for the receiving of the sacramental gifts in their initiation.

The fast on Friday and Saturday before the Pascha is the only fast that Hippolytus makes obligatory upon the whole Church. Other times of fasting are recommended both for clergy and laity, but are nonetheless voluntary. Hippolytus may have known—in fact, he must have known—of the weekly "stational" fasts of Wednesday and Friday, but he does not discuss them in the *Apostolic Tradition*. His silence on this subject implies, at least, that he did not consider them a matter of obligation. This is borne out by his specific directive that exempts the bishop from fasting "except when all the people fast also" (xxv, 2).

Hippolytus' conservatism on the matter of fasting is supported by the testimony of Tertullian. In his Montanist treatise *On Fasting* (2: 13), Tertullian castigated the Catholics for their laxity in making only the Paschal fast, "the days in which the Bridegroom is taken away" (cf. Mark 2: 20), an obligation, and all others a matter of choice. He cited the Catholic principle on this subject, that the only "solemnities" required for observance were those "appointed by the Scriptures or by the tradition of the ancients", and that no further innovations of observances should be added. With his characteristic sarcasm, he then accused the Catholics of breaking their own rule by extending the Paschal fast beyond the two days appointed and by their observance of the semi-fasts of the Stations, *i.e.*, Wednesdays and Fridays. But he testifies no less to the voluntary character of these extra ascetic devotions.[1]

The indication in Tertullian that Catholics in North Africa were already, in the early years of the third century, practising a more extensive Paschal fast than the traditional Friday and Saturday has an interesting confirmation in two documents of the middle of the century. The Syrian *Didascalia Apostolorum* directs churchmen to fast from the second through the fifth day of the week before the Pascha by taking only bread, salt, and water at the ninth hour (3 p.m.). "But on the Friday and on the Saturday fast wholly, and taste nothing."[2] Similarly, Dionysius of Alexandria, in his letter to Bishop Basilides that has already been noted, affirms that "all do not keep the six days of fasting either equally or in the same manner. But some pass all these days by remain-

---

times it was known as the *apertio aurium* or *Effeta*. See B. Botte, "Apertio aurium", *Reallexikon für Antike und Christentum* I, 487–9.

[1] Hippolytus himself roundly condemned a recent innovation of fasting on Saturdays. See his *Comm. in Dan.* iv, 20.

[2] Ch. 21 (ed. R. H. Connolly, 1929, p. 189).

ing without food altogether, while others observe only two days, others three or four days, and some not even one." However, all observe with rigor the fast of Friday and Saturday.[1]

The Paschal fast certainly had its roots in a period several generations before Hippolytus' time. The *Didache* (7: 4), though it does not specifically connect Baptism with the Pascha, contains the regulation that both the baptizer and the ones being baptized are to fast one or two days before the sacrament is administered. Justin Martyr is also witness to the custom:

> Those who are persuaded and believe that what is taught and said by us is true, and pledge themselves to be able to live accordingly, are taught to pray and beseech God, with fasting, for the forgiveness of their past sins, while we pray and fast along with them. Then they are brought by us to a place where there is water, and they are regenerated in the same manner in which we ourselves were regenerated.[2]

Lastly, there is the testimony of Irenaeus regarding the varied customs of the Paschal fast that were matters of dispute in the Quartodeciman controversy. The issues of the dispute, he said, did not have to do only with the day of the Pascha, "but with the very manner of the fast. For some think that they ought to fast a single day, others two, and others still more; while certain ones count forty hours of the day and night for their day (of fasting)."[3] This diversity, Irenaeus said, was not a recent thing, but had developed long before among "those who were antecedent to us".

(B) THE VIGIL

The liturgical celebration of the Pascha began with the all-night vigil that commenced after sundown on Saturday. Hippolytus says of it only that "they shall spend all the night in vigil, reading the Scriptures to them and instructing them". At cockcrow the vigil came to an end with the sacramental rites of initiation, and with them the fast was concluded. At least in Rome, the hour of cockcrow marked the decisive transition from fast to festival. But other churches began the festivities at an earlier hour in the evening. Dionysius of Alexandria, in his letter to Basilides, reprehended those who broke the fast before midnight, but he felt that the gospels did not give a clear indication of the exact

[1] Ed. by Feltoe, *op. cit.*, pp. 101-2.
[2] *Apol.* i, 61, 2-3.
[3] In Eusebius *H.E.* v, 24, 12.

hour of the Resurrection for those who wished to synchronize their devotion with the precise time of the Lord's rising from the dead.

The Alexandrian bishop showed some leniency towards those who because of their long fasting during the week felt the need of some refreshment before the vigil was over. We may suppose that they either brought some food with them to sustain them until the long ceremonies were over and the Paschal Eucharist finally ended, or that there were pauses or breaks within the course of the vigil itself.

The time of Hippolytus was doubtless much too early for there to have been developed a set schedule of scriptural readings for the vigil, such as one finds in the lectionary lists of post-Nicene sources. Dr. Anton Baumstark has called attention to the great similarity in the later lections assigned to the vigil in the rites of Jerusalem, Constantinople, Rome, and Milan, as also in the oldest surviving lectionary schemes of Gaul and Spain.[1] The pattern consisted of twelve lessons (the Byzantine rite has fifteen)—all from the Old Testament—and each list exhibits certain common material. The accounts of Creation, of Abraham's sacrifice of Isaac, of the Exodus Passover, of Jonah, and of the Three Children, occur in all of them; and common to several are the narratives of the Fall and of Jonah, the prophecies of Isaiah 55, and the Valley of Dry Bones of Ezekiel 37.

It is possible that behind this extraordinary agreement of later custom there lies a more ancient, pre-Nicene foundation. It is tempting to relate these lessons to some of the more popular representations of the biblical types of redemption-salvation found in the art of the catacombs.[2] On the other hand, it may well be that in this instance we have another example of the pervasive influence of the liturgical traditions developed in the church of Jerusalem in the fourth century, especially in the celebration of Holy Week and Easter. For among the extant sources, the lectionary scheme of Jerusalem is the only one that certainly reaches back to the fourth century.[3]

We may at least be certain that the narrative of the Exodus Passover was not only read, but also expounded, at the Paschal vigil in Hippolytus' time. This is attested by the homilies of Melito of Sardis,[4] of

[1] *Liturgie comparée* (3rd ed. by B. Botte, 1953), pp. 183 ff.

[2] Cf. W. Weidlé, *The Baptism of Art*, n.d., pp. 14 ff.

[3] F. C. Conybeare, *Rituale Armenorum*, 1905, pp. 516–27. It is also reproduced in M. L. McClure and C. L. Feltoe, *The Pilgrimage of Etheria* (Translations of Christian Literature, Series III: Liturgical Texts), n.d., pp. 78–9.

[4] Melito's homily begins: "The Scripture of the Hebrew Exodus has been read, and the words of the mystery have been interpreted, how the sheep is slain and how the people is saved." See edition of C. Bonner, *op. cit.*, pp. 86–7. Cf. G.

Origen, and of Hippolytus himself,[1] and the tradition is clearly indicated by Irenaeus.[2] If, as we believe, the fragment that concludes the *Epistle to Diognetus* is part of a Paschal sermon that dates from the same period, we may also conclude that the story of Adam and Eve in the Garden of Eden was another favored lesson of the vigil. A not insignificant support for this latter statement is the pictorial representation of Adam and Eve, the tree of knowledge, and the serpent, painted on the wall behind the baptistery of the house-church at Dura-Europos. This church was adapted for Christian worship not later than A.D. 232.[3] Another passage in the concluding fragment of the *Epistle to Diognetus* (11 : 6) suggests that a fourfold scheme of scriptural lessons made up the readings at the Pascha: the law, the prophets, the gospels, and the apostles.

(C) THE BAPTISM

When the hour arrived for baptizing the candidates, the ministers of the rite and the candidates repaired to the room of the house-church set apart as a baptistery. Hippolytus does not speak of this. But the arrangements of the house-church at Dura, mentioned above, make it clear that the baptisms were not administered in the face of the congregation of the faithful. Christian modesty alone would have rebelled at the notion that candidates stripped of their clothes and naked for the baptismal bath should have been exposed to the view of the entire church assembly.[4] We possess in any case the explicit testimony of Justin Martyr that, during the course of the baptisms, the faithful were engaged in common prayers, and that after the candidates

Zuntz, "On the Opening Sentence of Melito's Paschal Homily", *HTR* XXXVI, 1943, pp. 299–315; C. Bonner, "A Supplementary Note on the Opening of Melito's Homily", *ibid.*, 317–19.

[1] Cf. above, p. 50, note 2.

[2] *Adv. Haer.* iv, 20, 1 (ed. Harvey); also cf. his *Demonstration of the Apostolic Preaching*, 25.

[3] P. V. C. Baur and M. I. Rostovtzeff, *The Excavations at Dura-Europos*, Report V, 1934, p. 248.

[4] For this reason we cannot subscribe to the notion of G. Dix, *The Shape of the Liturgy*, 1945, p. 23, that "the tank of the *impluvium* would serve for the solemn immersion of baptism in the presence of the whole church". The *Didache* 7, 2 shows a distinct preference for the use of running water; and this appears also to be the case with Hippolytus (see the note in Dix's edition, p. 33). But Tertullian *De Baptismo* 4 distinctly affirms that it makes no difference whether the water of baptism is in "a sea or a pool, a river or a fountain, a lake or a tank".

had been initiated they were "escorted to the assembled brethren".[1]

Hippolytus' description of the baptismal rite is given with unusual fullness, with but one exception. It is strange that he provides no suggested form for blessing the water, though he directs that this be done first of all. According to Tertullian the blessing was an invocation of the Holy Spirit upon the water: "all waters . . . are consecrated as a mystery (*sacramentum*) of sanctification when God has been invoked; for immediately the Spirit comes from heaven and is upon the waters, sanctifying them of Himself, and they being themselves sanctified imbibe the power of sanctifying."[2] Our earliest extant forms of blessing of the water come only from the fourth century,[3] and these are likewise prayers of invocation. The Ethiopic version of the *Apostolic Tradition* contains three similar forms, of which the first, while it cannot be taken as an authentic expression of Hippolytus' writing, contains a petition of invocation that is fully in harmony with his theological thought: "stir this water and fill it up with thy Holy Spirit, that it may become water and Spirit for regeneration to those who are to be baptized."[4]

The directions of Hippolytus that the candidates should take off all their clothes—and for the women, remove all their jewelry, lest they go into the water wearing any "alien thing"—has been explained by Dr. W. C. van Unnik as a survival of Jewish custom in lustrations and proselyte baptism. It is not linked with the idea of demonic associations with objects worn on the body.[5]

More debated, however, has been the origin of the several anointings that accompanied the rite. Hippolytus speaks of two oils: an exorcized oil with which the candidates were anointed immediately after their renunciations of Satan and before their entrance into the water; and a consecrated oil "of thanksgiving" with which they were anointed after the baptismal bath. This latter oil of thanksgiving (*oleum sanctificatum*)

---

[1] *Apol.* i, 65, 1. Hippolytus implies the same, in his directive to the candidates after their baptism: "And so, each one drying himself, they shall put on their clothes and afterwards go in the assembly (*in ecclesia ingrediantur*)."

[2] *De Baptismo* 4.

[3] For Egypt, we have the *Sacramentary* of Sarapion, Bishop of Thmuis, where the blessing of the waters is definitely an invocation of the Logos. It is possible that such an invocation of the Logos is reflected in Clement of Alexandria, *Paed.* i, 6, 50. For Syria, the *Apostolic Constitutions* vii, 43 provides a form that reads: "Look down from heaven, and sanctify this water, and give it grace and power," etc. Cf. Ambrose, *De Mysteriis* 4 (19): "water does not cleanse without the Spirit."

[4] Edited by G. Horner, *op. cit.*, p. 165.

[5] "Les cheveux défaits des femmes baptisées. Un rite de Baptême dans l'Ordre ecclésiastique d'Hippolyte", *Vigiliae Christianae* I, 1947, pp. 77–100.

was also used by the bishop for an anointing after the laying on of hands that followed the baptism in water. Hippolytus refers to the same two unguents in his *Commentary on Daniel*,[1] where he gives them an allegorical interpretation (*i.e.*, they represent faith and charity with which the Church accompanies those who are baptized), and distinctly denotes the second oil as a perfumed ointment (myrrh). Tertullian speaks only of a single oil, the "blessed unction" (*benedicta unctio*) with which the baptized were anointed immediately after their coming forth from the font and before the laying on of hands of the bishop.[2] This oil must certainly correspond to the oil of thanksgiving mentioned by Hippolytus.

A generation later, Cyprian had occasion to mention the same unction after Baptism, which he described as "an oil sanctified on the altar".[3] This act of consecration of the unction, he said, took place at the Eucharist. For that reason he maintained that schismatics were incapable of administering a valid initiation, for having neither true church nor true altar they were incapable of providing a spiritual anointing by which the grace of Christ was conferred. The significant point here, for our purpose, is the observation that by Cyprian's time the act of anointing was considered as essential to the rite of initiation.

The Catholic Fathers were not the first, however, to mention anointing in connection with Baptism. It is related as being in use among some of the Gnostic groups. The earliest reference is contained in the excerpts made by Clement of Alexandria from the writings of Theodotus, a leader of the Oriental school of Valentinian Gnosticism.[4] Irenaeus also mentions its use among some of the Marcosians, a more degenerate company of Valentinians;[5] and Hippolytus refers to its practice among the Naassenes, one of the several varieties of Ophite Gnosticism.[6] This circumstance, plus the silence of second-century orthodox writers with respect to anointing, has led Dr. G. W. H. Lampe to the conclusion that the Gnostics gave such emphasis to the ceremony, even if they did not invent it, that orthodox Christians came to give it a significance all their own.[7] Dom Gregory Dix was

---

[1] i, 16 (ed. G. Bardy, with text and translation by M. Lefevre, *Hippolyte, Commentaire sur Daniel*, Sources chrétiennes, 1947, p. 101).

[2] Ch. 7.

[3] *Epist.* lxx, 2.

[4] F. Sagnard, *Clément d'Alexandrie, Extraits de Théodote* (Sources chrétiennes), 1948, pp. 199–213, 229–39.

[5] *Adv. Haer.* i, 21, 4.

[6] *Philos.* v, 7.

[7] *The Seal of the Spirit*, 1951, pp. 120–9.

emphatically of the contrary opinion, maintaining that Valentinus retained for his followers in this instance a ceremony already traditional in the Church.[1]

Arguments from silence are never very convincing either way. We may affirm that the New Testament provides no certain indication of a ceremony of anointing or chrismation in Christian initiation. The two principal passages that refer to believers being anointed or having an anointing (2 Cor. 1: 21 and 1 John 2: 20, 27) have nothing to do with a rite, but refer to the share which the Christians have in Christ, the true "Anointed One" of God.[2] And it is this significance that Tertullian and Cyprian give to the later ceremony of anointing, as a symbol of the Christian's participation in the Priesthood and Messiahship of their Lord. It is possible that the biblical concepts (including, for example, 1 Peter 2: 5, 9 and Rev. 1: 6) suggested the adoption of the ceremony of anointing. But there may well be a simpler explanation at hand. The ancients associated anointing, with perfumed unguents, with bathing. A formal bath, such as Baptism, would ordinarily be completed in this way. Thus a common custom, carried over into the Church's usage, would lend itself upon reflection to spiritual or mystical interpretations. Both the orthodox and the heretics would develop this symbolism in their own ways, though not without some interaction of influence each upon the other.[3]

The order of the rite of Baptism as laid out by Hippolytus progressed as follows:

(1) The candidate recited his formal renunciations of Satan, his service and his works.

(2) He was then anointed with the oil of exorcism, while the presbyter pronounced: "Let all evil spirits depart far from thee."

(3) He descended into the font, with a deacon who assisted him.

(4) The one who baptized then interrogated the candidate as to his belief, in the words of a creed. After each of the three sections of the creed, the candidate affirmed, "I believe". And each time he was baptized while the baptizer laid his hand upon the candidate's head.

(5) When the candidate came up from the water, he was anointed with the oil of thanksgiving by the presbyter.

(6) He then dried himself, put on his clothes, and with the other initiates returned to the assembly of the church.

[1] See his edition of the *Apostolic Tradition, op. cit.,* p. xxxix.
[2] Lampe, *op. cit.,* pp. 6–7.
[3] See the Appended Note to this chapter.

The renunciations of Satan, the professions of faith ("somewhat more amply than the Lord determined in the gospel"), and the trine immersion are all mentioned by Tertullian, who also denotes the bishop as the baptizing minister.[1] There are, however, no earlier testimonies to the renunciations. But the professions of faith go back, of course, to apostolic times, developing from simple formulas such as the confession that "Jesus is Lord" to the credal formulations of the second century. Hippolytus is one of our important witnesses to the form of the old Roman Creed, commonly called today the Apostles' Creed.[2] An interesting early second-century example of profession of faith at Baptism is afforded by the "western" text of Acts 8: 36–7:

> And the eunuch said, "Behold, water! What prevents my being baptized?" And Philip said to him, "If you believe with your whole heart, it is possible." And he answered, "I believe that Jesus Christ is the Son of God."

One should also note that the custom of trine immersion, corresponding to the threefold profession of the Name of Father, Son, and Holy Spirit, is attested as early as the *Didache* (7: 3).

What is perhaps the more remarkable circumstance in Hippolytus' description is the absence of the formula "In the Name of the Father, and of the Son, and of the Holy Spirit," said by the minister of Baptism. It may be implied in his directives, but it is not explicitly stated. The same ambiguity surrounds the notices of Tertullian. The statement of the latter in his *Against Praxeas* (26) that "not once, but thrice, we are baptized unto each several Person at each several Name" suggests that in North Africa, as at Rome, the response of the candidate to the "more ample" credal formula was considered to be equivalent to the recital of the threefold Name by the minister.[3] The earlier texts of the second century, however, imply that the minister himself recited over the candidate the threefold Name. This is true of both orthodox and Gnostic sources.[4]

---

[1] Especially *De spect.* 4, 24; *De corona* 3. For full references and discussion of Tertullian's evidence, see E. Dekkers, *Tertullianus en de Geschiedenis der Liturgie*, 1947, pp. 163 ff.; also R. F. Refoulé and M. Drouzy, *Tertullien, Traité du Baptême* (Sources chrétiennes), 1952, pp. 29–45.

[2] See the excellent discussion of J. N. D. Kelly, *Early Christian Creeds*, 1950, pp. 1–130.

[3] See Dekkers, *op. cit.*, pp. 189–91.

[4] *Didache* 7, 1; Justin Martyr *Apol.* i, 61 (where the formula is somewhat expanded); Clement of Alexandria, *Exc. ex. Theod.* 80; Irenaeus *Adv. Haer.* i, 21, 3 (the varied expanded formulas used by some of the Gnostics).

Tertullian mentions one custom not noted in Hippolytus. The initiates refrained from taking their daily bath for a week after their Baptism.[1] We may see here the germ of the "octave" of the Pascha that is so important in the later liturgies of the fourth century. But there is no indication in Tertullian as yet of the white garments given to the baptized which they were to wear during this octave.[2]

(D) THE CONFIRMATION[3]

The Confirmation of the baptized by the bishop immediately following the ceremonies of the font was held in the presence of all the people. It consisted of four actions:

(1) The laying on of hands with prayer.
(2) The anointing on the head with the consecrated oil (chrism).
(3) The sealing on the forehead, i.e., marking the sign of the cross.
(4) The kiss of peace.

Following this, the initiates participated for the first time in the prayers of the faithful, exchanged with them the kiss of peace, and joined in the offertory action for which they had brought for the first time their oblations of bread and wine. But this anticipates the discussion of the Paschal Eucharist.

We need not enter at this point into the much-canvassed and long-disputed questions regarding the "relation of Baptism and Confirmation", the particular moment of the gift of the Holy Spirit, and the exact meaning of the word "seal" so commonly associated with the rite of initiation. For the Fathers did not think of the Paschal mystery as a series of distinct sacraments, but took the whole complex of rites and ceremonies as a whole. One may find a thorough survey of the relevant material in Dr. Lampe's work, to which reference has been made, even if one does not always agree with his interpretations of the sources.

That the rite of laying on of hands in close proximity to Baptism was practised in the apostolic age cannot be disputed. What is in question is the meaning of this act as it appears from time to time in the narrative of Acts. In the case of St. Paul's initiation at Damascus (Acts 9: 17–18), the laying on of hands by Ananias may have been nothing other than an

---

[1] De corona 3.
[2] Cf. Dekkers, op. cit., pp. 210–12; A. Kurfess and A. Hermann, "Candidatus",. Reallexikon für Antike und Christentum II, 840–1.
[3] We do not use the word "Confirmation" here as implying in any way a sacrament distinct from Baptism, but adopt the later terminology of the Church solely as a convenience for analysis.

act of healing, and not necessarily part of the initiation. The crucial passages are those relating the laying on of hands upon the Samaritans baptized by Philip through the personal intervention of the apostles Peter and John (Acts 8: 17), and the laying on of hands immediately following Baptism upon the Ephesian disciples through the ministration of the apostle Paul (Acts 19: 6). The Evangelist does not make clear whether these acts of imposition of hands are a completion of initiation by the gift of the Spirit—as seems more likely at Samaria—or are a special gift of the Spirit for extraordinary charismata, such as speaking in tongues—as seems more likely at Ephesus. Irenaeus in one place[1] and Tertullian in several scattered passages appear to have been the first of the Fathers to link the narratives of Acts with the idea that the primary gift of the Spirit is imparted through the laying on of hands. But their language, when taken in total perspective of all they have to say about initiation, is by no means consistent.[2]

In his work *On Baptism* (8), Tertullian distinctly says, "then a hand is laid (upon us) for a benediction, invoking and inviting the Holy Spirit". He does not give us a form of the prayer. Unfortunately, the form of prayer at the imposition of hands in Hippolytus' *Apostolic Tradition* is subject to dispute with regard to its text. The Latin version —generally more reliable—reads:

> O Lord God, who hast made these worthy to deserve the forgiveness of sins through the laver of regeneration of the Holy Spirit; send upon them thy grace that they may serve thee according to thy will; for to thee is the glory, to the Father and the Son with the Holy Spirit in the holy Church both now and for ever. Amen.

The other versions, which Dom Gregory Dix prefers in his edition, make the petition read, "Make them worthy to be filled with thy Holy Spirit and send upon them thy grace", etc. Dr. Lampe is probably right in preferring the Latin to the Oriental versions, for it is easier to explain the latter as responsive to the theological theories of later times.[3]

Another disputed point concerns the anointing. In Hippolytus, the chrismation by the bishop takes place after the laying on of hands, and is distinctly different from the anointing with the oil of thanksgiving immediately after the baptismal bath. But Tertullian in his work *On Baptism* mentions only one anointing, and this one occurs before the laying on of hands. Scholars have disagreed as to whether the chrisma-

[1] *Adv. Haer.* iv, 38, 2; cf. Lampe, *op. cit.*, p. 118.
[2] Cf. the survey of Tertullian in Lampe, *op. cit.*, pp. 157–62.
[3] *Op. cit.*, pp. 136–41; so also B. S. Easton, *op. cit.*, p. 47.

tion in Tertullian's account belongs to the Baptism or to the Confirmation.[1] If the chrismation belongs to Confirmation, then the order of ceremonies in North Africa was the reverse of that at Rome.

Tertullian is also a witness to the ceremony of signing the mark of the cross on the forehead. In an interesting passage of his work *Against Marcion* (iii, 22), he relates this sign—the letter Tau that is the very form of the cross—to the prophecy of Ezekiel 9: 4.[2] It is noteworthy, too, that he mentions this ceremony as in use among the Marcionites along with "the sacraments of the Church".

(E) THE EUCHARIST

Only two points about the Paschal Eucharist as outlined by Hippolytus call for special comment. It has already been noted that immediately after the Confirmation of the initiates, the liturgy proceeded at once to the eucharistic rite, beginning with the prayers of the faithful and the kiss of peace. Then followed the offertory. Exactly the same order is described by Justin Martyr.[3] That is to say, the Paschal Eucharist, unlike the regular Sunday Eucharist, does not begin with the readings from Scripture and the sermon. These were doubtless considered unnecessary in view of the lessons and sermon of the vigil. One might hazard the conjecture that the same distinction between a Eucharist following Baptism and a Sunday Eucharist is suggested by the *Didache* if one compares chapters 9–10 with chapter 14 of this document.

A special feature of the Paschal Eucharist was the preparation of three chalices instead of one for the communion. Hippolytus notes, in addition to the regular chalice of wine, a cup of mingled honey and milk, and a cup of water. The cup of honey and milk is a type of the Promised Land, the cup of water is a sign of the laver of Baptism. Both Clement of Alexandria[4] and Tertullian[5] are witnesses to the custom of the cup of honey and milk; and Clement gives it much the same explanation as does Hippolytus. Less certain is the testimony of Justin Martyr.[6] He speaks of an offering at the baptismal Eucharist of a "cup

---

[1] Cf. Dekkers, *op. cit.*, pp. 198–200.

[2] Origen, *Selecta in Ezek.* ix, says that the reference to the letter Tau in Ezek. 9: 4 occurs, not in the LXX, but in the versions of Aquila and Theodotion. He also relates it to the Christian custom of making the sign of the cross, but he does not speak of it in connection with initiation.

[3] *Apol.* i, 65.

[4] *Paed.* i, 6, 34 ff.

[5] *De corona* 3; *Adv. Marc.* i, 14; cf. Dekkers, *op. cit.*, pp. 205–7.

[6] *Apol.* i, 65, 3.

of water and mixture". Most commentators take this to mean a single chalice of wine mixed with water. But it is a curious expression even so, especially since his description of the Sunday Eucharist specifically mentions the offering of "wine and water". It is possible that Justin refers to two cups, one of water and another of wine mixed with water. It is less likely that his "mixture" is a cup of honey and milk.[1]

APPENDED NOTE

The Pascha in Second Century Gnosticism

1. *The Marcionites.* The evidence is supplied by Tertullian and suggests that the Marcionite liturgy did not differ in any important way from that of the Catholics. In *Against Marcion* i, 14, he says that Marcion did not reprove "the water of the Creator whereby He washes them, nor the oil wherewith He anoints them, nor the mingling of the honey and milk with which He nourishes them as children, nor the bread by which He represents His own Body". The outline of the Paschal celebration is very clear from this statement. Then in iii. 22, Tertullian reminds the Marcionites that not only did Christ suffer, but He foretold that His faithful ones would suffer also. Thus He signed them with that Tau, the form of the cross, of which Ezekiel (9: 4) prophesied. "For that letter Tau of the Greeks, which is moreover our T, the form of the cross, is what he predicted would be in the future on our foreheads in the true and catholic Jerusalem." After further citations of Old Testament prophecies, Tertullian concludes, "Since all these things are also found among you, the signing of the forehead and the sacraments of the Church and the pure offerings of sacrifices, you ought now to break forth and declare that the Spirit of the Creator prophesied of your Christ."

Since Tertullian gives no indication of any major difference between the Marcionites and the Catholics in these matters, we may conclude one of two positions. Either these customs go back to the early part of the second century, prior to the expulsion of Marcion from the Catholic Church, or they were adopted by the Marcionites after their schism in deliberate imitation of the Catholic Church. The latter is the less likely position, for, as Tertullian does not fail to note, the use of "beggarly" material elements in the worship of the

---

[1] One of the MSS. omits the reference to the mixed cup. This is too slender a basis for the theory of Harnack, also advanced by Lietzmann, that Justin is a witness to eucharistic celebrations with bread and water only. See the comments in A. Arnold, *Der Ursprung des christlichen Abendmahls* (Freiburger theologische Studien, Heft 45), 1937, pp. 30–1.

Marcionites was in contradiction to their views about the evil of matter. Irenaeus used similar arguments against the Gnostics.

On the basis of *Against Marcion* i, 19, Harnack reckoned that the rupture of Marcion with the Roman Church took place in July, A.D. 144. This dating has been generally accepted by most critics. According to the Chronicle of Edessa (*c.* 540), Marcion left the Catholic Church in A.D. 138.

2. *The Naassenes.* Our only source is the *Refutation of All Heresies* (also known as the *Philosophumena* or the *Elenchos*), attributed by most modern scholars to Hippolytus. For his description of them, Hippolytus enjoyed original sources. The Naassenes were a very syncretistic Gnostic group of the Ophite type. The principal document that Hippolytus used was a commentary by an unnamed Gnostic theologian upon a hymn to Attis. It is a strange and curious mixture of mythology and exegesis, and not often very clear in the progress of its exposition. But there can be no doubt that an initiation ceremony modelled upon the Church's rite was a central feature of the Naassenes' mysteries.

After citing Romans 1: 20-8, the interpreter maintained that "in these words that Paul has spoken, there is comprised their whole secret and the unspeakable mystery of blessed pleasure. For the promise of the laver is not anything else, according to them, than the leading to unfading pleasure of him who has been washed in living water and anointed with other (or, according to a commonly accepted emendation, ineffable) ointment" (v, 7). Again, towards the conclusion of Hippolytus' excerpt, it is stated, "We are the spiritual, who have chosen what is ours, out of the living water—the Euphrates which flows through the midst of Babylon—in entering through the true gate which is Jesus the blessed. And we Christians alone of all men are those whom the mystery in the third gate has made perfect, and are anointed there with the ineffable ointment from the horn, such as that with which David was anointed" (v, 9).

In between these two passages there runs a flow of comment that curiously interweaves the Old Testament narrative of the Exodus and entrance across Jordan into the promised land with citations from Homer. And all of this is interpreted in the light of the new birth from water and the Spirit of John 3: 5-6. Of particular interest in our inquiry are the references in this section to the eating of the Saviour's flesh and the drinking of His blood, and to the tasting of honey and milk. However bizarre the interpretations, it is apparent that the Naassenes had an initiatory rite of similar ceremonies to those of the orthodox. It is hard to believe, in any case, that in this instance the Catholics would have been the borrowers.

3. *The Valentinians.* The primary source is the concluding section (76-86) of the *Excerpts from Theodotus*, made by Clement of Alexandria. Here again, the initiatory rite of the Church is described by way of a theological commentary, albeit one far more consistent and unified than what one finds in the Naassenes' document. We are dealing with an early phase of Valentinian Gnosis, before its basic myth had become degenerated and confused. The material probably dates from the third quarter of the second century. It may be best to present it

by way of excerpts from the *Excerpts*, leaving aside so far as possible the peculiar Valentinian exegesis. We use the helpful edition and commentary by F. Sagnard in *Sources chrétiennes*.

"In the same way in which the birth of the Saviour has delivered us from Becoming and from Fate, so His Baptism has delivered us from fire, and His suffering from suffering, in order that we might follow Him in all things. For he who has been baptized unto God has advanced toward God and received 'power to tread upon scorpions and serpents', that is, the evil Powers. And He commanded His apostles: 'Go forth and preach; and baptize those who believe in the Name of the Father and the Son and the Holy Spirit,' in whom we are regenerated, being made superior to all the rest of the Powers." . . .

"And they have died to the world, but live unto God, in order that death might be destroyed by death, and corruption by resurrection. For he who has been sealed by the Father and the Son and the Holy Spirit is no more subject to any other power; but by the three Names there is deliverance from the whole Triad of corruption. 'He who bears the image of the earthly shall then bear the image of the heavenly.' " . . .

"Baptism is analogously twofold: sensible, by water; . . . intelligible, by Spirit." . . .

"And the bread and the oil are sanctified by the power of God's Name . . . and by this power they are transformed into spiritual power. Likewise also the water, when it is exorcized and becomes Baptism, not only separates the inferior, but also acquires sanctification.

"It is fitting to come to Baptism rejoicing. But since often there descend with them (into the water) unclean spirits, accompanying and obtaining the seal with man, so that they become incorrigible later, fear is mixed with joy, so that only a clean person should come. Hence there are fasts, supplications, prayers, (impositions of) hands, genuflexions, that the soul may be saved from the world and 'from the mouth of lions.' " . . .

The similarity of initiation among the Valentinians to that described by Hippolytus is herewith apparent, even to the disciplines of catechetical preparation. Though the Eucharist is referred to only incidentally by way of "the bread", it is most certainly part of the rite. And with the exception of the reference to the oil, there is nothing in this order that is not mentioned or implied in the writings of Justin Martyr.

4. *The Marcosians.* This group of Gnostics take their name from a Valentinian charlatan named Marcus, whose ideas and practices came to the particular notice of Irenaeus (*Adv. Haer.* i, 13 ff.). There seem to have been diversities among them in their rites. In Book I, chapter 21, Irenaeus recounts some of them with respect to Baptism. The several varieties are as follows:

(*a*) A mystic marriage, instead of Baptism—possibly by analogy with some of the initiatory ceremonies of the mystery cults.

(*b*) Baptism in water with the use of formulas expanding the triune Name with varied divine names dear to Gnostic speculation and mythology.

(*c*) Baptism by a mixture of oil and water poured on the head of the candidates, with varied formulas such as those used by the (*b*) group. "This they wish to be redemption. And they also anoint with balsam."

(*d*) Rejection of all material and external elements and ceremonies. "Perfect redemption is none other than Gnosis itself of the ineffable Greatness."

It is clear from Irenaeus' account that the Marcosians were not inventors of new rites and ceremonies so much as adapters of rites and ceremonies already known. They have nothing to contribute to a knowledge of the origin and development of the Church's initiatory liturgy.

V

THE PASCHA IN PRIVATE DEVOTION

Throughout the "age of persecution", the piety of the Church, both official and unofficial, maintained an eschatological orientation. Its life was in "the last times", its true citizenship in heaven, the expected age to come. So its corporate observance was pivoted in the Paschal commemoration of death and resurrection, with its weekly renewal on Sundays. These alone were days of obligation for all the faithful, for participation in the eucharistic banquet, which was the earnest of the awaited consummation.

Yet there were other days and times of particular devotion, voluntary in character, though highly recommended for the cultivation of piety. And these also came to take on the spirit of Paschal commemoration. Most striking was the development of devotion to the martyrs, on the anniversaries of their triumphs. These, too, were days of death and resurrection; and for those who were able to observe them they were marked by a eucharistic feast such as to make them, like Sundays, another reminder of the Pascha of the Lord. Where possible, the commemoration took place at the tomb-shrines where the relics or remains of the martyrs lay buried.

The earliest reference to such observances comes from the account of Polycarp's martyrdom at Smyrna in the year 155 or 156. "We took up his bones, more precious than costly stones and more valuable than gold, and laid them away in a suitable place," says the communication of the church in Smyrna. "There the Lord will permit us, so far as possible, to gather together in joy and gladness to celebrate the day of his martyrdom as a birthday, in memory of those athletes who have gone before, and to train and make ready those who are to come hereafter."[1] Tertullian testifies to these *natalicia*, or "birthdays", as a tradition in North Africa in his time, and in addition speaks of "oblations" offered by the faithful on the anniversaries of their departed loved ones.[2]

[1] *Mart. Poly.* 18.
[2] Especially *De corona* 3. See the full discussion, with many other references, in A. C. Rush, *Death and Burial in Christian Antiquity* (Studies in Christian Antiquity No. 1), 1941, pp. 72–87.

Cyprian was careful to keep a record of the dates of death of the martyrs and confessors that he might offer the customary commemorative Eucharists.[1] At Rome, the cultus of the martyrs seems to have been first officially systematized by Pope Fabian (236–50), martyred himself in the Decian persecution. It was Fabian who constructed the special crypt for the Roman bishops in what later came to be known as the Catacomb of Callistus.[2]

(A) THE WEEKLY STATIONS

The Paschal celebration reacted upon the weekly observance of Wednesdays and Fridays, as days of special devotion, that began to spread throughout the churches in the second century. In the Western Church, these days were known as "stations".[3] But our earliest references to them come from the East, where they developed as days of fasting and prayer. The *Didache* (8: 1) recommends them after the manner of the Jewish fast days of Mondays and Thursdays, but is particular to remind its readers that the Christian devotion should select Wednesdays and Fridays so as not to coincide with the Jewish days. Clement of Alexandria, on the other hand, sees these days as appropriate for Christian fasts from money and pleasure, since the pagans associated Wednesdays and Fridays with Hermes (Mercury) and Aphrodite (Venus), respectively.[4]

It is probable that most churches provided corporate worship on these station days. Tertullian speaks of a celebration of the Eucharist at a morning hour.[5] But this may have been a peculiarity of the North African Church. For neither at Rome nor at Alexandria was there a tradition of eucharistic celebrations on these days as late as the fifth century. Instead, there was a synaxis, a gathering for the reading and exposition of the Scriptures.[6] Origen even implies a daily synaxis at Caesarea during his years there as teacher, preacher, and priest.[7] Hippolytus, curiously, does not mention the station days specifically, though

---

[1] *Ep.* xii, 2; xxxix, 3.

[2] Cf. E. Caspar, *Geschichte des Papsttums*, 1930, I, 50.

[3] See the exhaustive study of the origin and meaning of this word by C. Mohrmann, "Statio", *Vigiliae Christianae* VII, 1953, pp. 221–45.

[4] *Strom.* vii, 12, 75–6.

[5] *De orat.* 19.

[6] Socrates *H.E.* v, 22; Innocent I, *Ep. ad Decentium* 7. Cf. L. Duchesne, *Origines du culte chrétien*, 5th ed., 1925, p. 243.

[7] *Hom. in Gen.* x, 2–3; *Hom. in Jes. Nav.* iv, 1.

he speaks of voluntary fasts,[1] and notes that on certain weekdays there was an "instruction" at the place where the church assembled.[2] Though Origen castigated many of his listeners for not attending more often than on feast days, it is clear that these week-day assemblies were not of obligation in the way the Sunday Eucharist was required of all the faithful. Indeed, Tertullian as a Montanist criticized the Catholics because even the fasts of the station days were voluntary.[3]

Tertullian is the earliest writer to relate the stational fasts in any way to a commemoration of the Lord's Passion. He states that the Catholics ended their fast on these days at the ninth hour, i.e., 3 p.m., because that was the hour of the Lord's death, when the period of darkness was lifted once more into the sunshine of the day. As a Montanist, however, he preferred to prolong his fast until sundown, the time of the Lord's burial.[4] Only later in the third century were the station days more specifically made commemorations of the Betrayal (Wednesdays) and the Crucifixion (Fridays). For the East, we have the testimony of the *Didascalia Apostolorum*, a mid-century document from Syria.[5] In the West, a similar association was made by Victorinus of Pettau (d. 304).[6]

Thus each week came to be a renewal of Holy Week, as each Sunday was a renewal of the Pascha. And it may be that the custom of extending the Friday fast to include Saturday—a practice that had its beginnings in the time of Tertullian and Hippolytus, but only became established in the church at Rome[7]—was a further extension of the association of the weekly commemorations with the annual days of the Paschal rites.

(B) DAILY HOURS OF PRAYER

The first Christians inherited from their Jewish devotion the custom of offering prayers at certain fixed times of the day. These were generally appointed at the hours of the chief sacrifices in the Temple. As the gospel spread to the Gentile world, the hours of prayer came to be associated with the customary time divisions of Graeco-Roman daily life. By the latter part of the second century, the round of daily

[1] *Apostolic Tradition* xxvii.
[2] *Ibid.*, xxxi, xxxv–vi.
[3] *De ieiunio* 2, 10.
[4] *Ibid.*, 10.
[5] Ch. 21 (ed. R. H. Connolly, p. 184).
[6] *De fabr. mundi* 3–4.
[7] Tertullian *De ieiunio* 14; Hippolytus *Comm. in Dan.* iv, 20. For later Roman practice, see Augustine *Ep.* xxxvi, 32; liv, 2.

prayer among the devout had become traditional at the following periods:

> Morning, upon arising at daybreak
> The third hour (9 a.m.)
> The sixth hour (noon)
> The ninth hour (3 p.m.)
> Evening, upon retiring to bed
> Midnight.

With minor variations, these hours of prayer are noted in the writings of Clement and Origen, Hippolytus, Tertullian and Cyprian. They are, of course, the basis of the later Canonical Hours of the ascetics and monks.[1]

Already by the turn of the second-third centuries the hours of prayer were being recommended by associating them with events in the life of the Lord or the Apostles, no less than with the example of Daniel (6: 10) and the psalmists of the Old Testament. Both Tertullian[2] and Origen[3] relate them specifically to "apostolic" practice as recorded in the Book of Acts. But the round of daily prayer as laid out by Hippolytus[4] has a peculiar interest for our purpose, because it is entirely integrated into a commemorative sequence of the Passion and Resurrection of Christ. This sequence, it may be noted, conforms exactly to Roman time reckoning, and follows the pattern of the Passion narrative as it is recorded in the "Roman "gospel, namely that according to St. Mark.

Actually Hippolytus has seven, not six, times of daily prayer, and these form two groups. One group has no special association with the gospel story: namely, the morning prayer, when one arises at dawn from sleep and prepares to go to the day's work; and the evening prayer, before one retires to bed. Presumably these two times of prayer are expected of all Christians in any case. It is the other group, at particularly noted times, that provides the extra "ascetical" effort. The commemorative symbolism of these hours may be schematized as follows:

---

[1] A convenient summary of the development will be found in C. W. Dugmore, *The Influence of the Synagogue Upon the Divine Office*, 1944, chapter IV. The principal texts are collected in E. G. Jay, *Origen's Treatise on Prayer*, 1954, pp. 36-41.

[2] *De orat.* 25; cf. *De ieiunio* 10.

[3] *De orat.* xii, 2.

[4] *Apostolic Tradition* xxxv-vi.

Third Hour: Christ was nailed to the tree.
The shewbread of the Old Covenant was offered.
The Paschal lamb was slain.

Sixth Hour: Christ was hanged on the wood.
Darkness covered the earth.
Cry of Christ on the Cross.

Ninth Hour: Christ died and descended into Hades.
Christ's side was pierced.
Daylight reappears.

Midnight: All creation is hushed for a moment of praise to God.
The time of Christ's expected return—the cry of the
coming of the Bridegroom.

Cockcrow: The Jews denied Christ.
The resurrection.

Within the course of twenty-four hours, two cycles of commemoration are thus interwoven by Hippolytus. From cockcrow to cockcrow, the course of the Passion is followed from the condemnation of Jesus by the Sanhedrin in the early morning hours before He was delivered to Pilate, to the pre-dawn resurrection of the Lord. For "cockcrow" was the time especially associated by the Roman Church with the resurrection.[1] But there was also a recalling, within the twenty-four hour period, of the three days from death to resurrection. This was made possible by counting the three hours of darkness, from noon to 3 p.m., as a night separating two days. So the first day lasted from the Jews' denial to the noon darkness; the second day, from the reappearance of the light at the ninth hour until sundown; the third day opened with the resurrection at cockcrow. The same scheme occurs in the *Didascalia Apostolorum*[2] where the sequence of the Passion follows more closely the Johannine rather than the Markan narrative:

They crucified Him on the same Friday. He suffered, then, at the sixth hour on Friday. And these hours wherein our Lord was crucified were reckoned a day. And afterwards, again, there was darkness for three hours; and it was reckoned a night. And again, from the ninth hour until evening, three hours, (reckoned) a day. And afterwards again, (there was) the night of the Sabbath of the Passion. . . . And again (there was) the day of the Sabbath; and then three hours of the night after the Sabbath, wherein our Lord slept.

Another commemorative mark of the Pascha is associated by Hippo-

[1] Cf. Dionysius of Alexandria *Ep. ad Basilidem* (ed. C. L. Feltoe, pp. 94–5).
[2] Ch. 21 (ed. R. H. Connolly, p. 182).

lytus with the hours of prayer by his comments on the sign of the cross. His remarks come to us in two recensions of the extant text of the *Apostolic Tradition*, In the first notice, he speaks of the sign at the time of the midnight prayer, where it recalls the initiation of the Christian:

> By signing thyself with the moist breath and catching thy breath in the hand, thy body is sanctified even to thy feet. For so the gift of the Spirit and the sprinkling of the font, when it is offered with a believing heart, as it were from a fountain, sanctifies him who believes.[1]

The second comment comes at the conclusion of the outline of hours of prayer. It specifically links the sign of the cross with the "sign of the Passion", and is used as a shield against the devil's wiles. "And so the Adversary, seeing the power of the Spirit made manifest from the heart in the image of Baptism, is terrified and flees—not because of thy striking him, but because of thy breathing (on him)."[2]

The consistency of Hippolytus' integration of the hours of prayer with Paschal commemoration was not maintained by later writers. The memories of the Passion were fused with other associations, notably those of apostolic observance in the Book of Acts. The reason probably lies in the preference for the Johannine narrative, over against Mark, as well as in the general tendency to enlarge rather than to restrict the content of devotional subjects. An excellent illustration is provided by Cyprian, who conflates three strands of devotion in his comments upon the day-hours at nine, noon, and three o'clock. First, there is his own idea of linking the three-hour periods with the mystery of the Trinity. Secondly, there is the inherited North African scheme already known to Tertullian. The third hour recalls the descent of the Spirit upon the Apostles, the sixth hour the prayer of Peter on the house-top. He does not, however, go on, as did Tertullian, to associate the ninth hour with the prayer of Peter and John in the Temple and the healing of the lame man at the Beautiful Gate. Instead, he recalls the crucifixion of the Lord that lasted from the sixth to the ninth hour.[3]

Cyprian's mention of other periods of prayer also reveals the conflation of varying traditions. Morning prayers are a celebration of the resurrection; evening prayers are reminders that Christ is the true Sun and Day and Light, hence look forward to the coming again of His light in the Second Advent. The same theme of light is carried over to

---

[1] xxxvi, 11 (Latin version; ed. G. Dix, p. 66).
[2] xxxvii, 1–2 (Latin version "a"; ed. G. Dix, p. 69).
[3] *De dom. orat.* 35.

his remarks about prayers during the night, with a specific mention of the example of the widow Anna.[1]

Later monastic writers exhibit the same conflation. St. Basil recommends the canonical hours by reference to the Psalms and Acts.[2] Cassian uses the same sources, but also recalls the crucifixion at noon and the descent into Hades at the ninth hour. He links Vespers with the institution of the Eucharist.[3] Yet the Hippolytean tradition was not entirely obscured or forgotten, but survived in the metrical mediaeval hymns of the Passion, of which the most famous was the fourteenth-century *Patris sapientia*. A synopsis of its commemoration is represented in the verses:

> At *Mattins* bound, at *Prime* reviled,
>   Condemned to death at *Tierce*,
> Nailed to the Cross at *Sext*, at *Nones*
>   His blessed side they pierce.
>
> They take Him down at *Vesper-tide*,
>   In grave at *Compline* lay;
> Who thenceforth bids His Church observe
>   Her sevenfold hours alway.

[1] *Ibid.*, 36.
[2] *Regulae Fusius Tractatae* xxxvii, 383–4.
[3] *Inst.* iii, 3.

Part Two

THE PASCHAL LITURGY
IN THE APOCALYPSE

VI

THE STRUCTURE OF THE BOOK OF REVELATION

THE ANALYSIS of the Book of Revelation herewith to be presented makes a very modest claim with respect to its liturgical origins. We do not propose the thesis that the Apocalypse is either a liturgy or a lectionary, or even a liturgical homily. Without question the book is a work of prophecy. Whatever may have been the Jewish or non-Christian sources that the Seer has utilized or re-worked, his book as we have it is a prophecy of Christian inspiration, penetrating and powerful in its vision and imagery, celebrating the ultimate victory of Christ and of His saints over all the powers of evil.

We adopt the view most commonly held by critics, that the work was composed in the last years of the reign of Domitian, in the province of Asia. Its author had some relation to the theological thought of the Gospel and Epistles ascribed to John, but he was not by any means the author or source of any of these other "Johannine" writings.

The thesis here presented has to do primarily with the structure of the Apocalypse. We propose to show that the outline or plan according to which the visions unfold is possibly—we would say, probably—laid out in a scheme that follows the order of the Church's Paschal liturgy. It has always been recognized that Revelation contains in its hymns and anthems an abundance of liturgical material. The theological significance of this material has been the subject of an acute discussion by Erik Peterson.[1] In particular, chapters 4 and 5 have been studied with a view towards illuminating the liturgical setting of the Seer's visions and illustrating certain liturgical usages of the early Church.[2] But none of

---

[1] *Das Buch von den Engeln, Stellung und Bedeutung der heiligen Engel im Kultus*, 1935. I am familiar only with the Italian translation by R. Giachino, *Il libro degli Angeli*, 1946.

[2] Otto A. Piper, "The Apocalypse of John and the Liturgy of the Ancient Church", *Church History* XX, 1951, pp. 10–22; Lucetta Mowry, "Revelation 4–5 and Early Christian Liturgical Usage", *JBL* LXXI, 1952, pp. 75–84; A. Feuillet, "Les vingt-quatre vieillards de l'Apocalypse", *Revue Biblique* LXV, 1958, especially p. 11.

these studies has attempted to place the overall design of the Apocalypse within a liturgical framework. An exception to this statement may possibly be made in view of the erudite if no less curious exposition of Austin Farrer.[1]

Our study was worked out independently of Dr. Farrer's book. The primary value of his analysis, in our opinion, is the skill with which he exhibits the transformation of Jewish festival symbolism in the visions of the Seer—the remarkable fusion in the Apocalypse of the ceremonial imagery associated with the successive feasts of Tabernacles, Dedication, Passover, and Pentecost. But the calendrical scheme, if one may call it such, that Dr. Farrer works out with such intricacy and diligence, is too contrived. The result of his labor is to give an exegesis of Revelation that is more complicated than the book itself. One needs a commentary to Dr. Farrer's commentary. For our purpose, we have found more satisfactory the main outlines of exposition and commentary in Dr. R. H. Charles' great work.[2] But we have not found it necessary to our purpose to adopt the transpositions of the text that Dr. Charles has recommended.

The clue that led us to our theory about the structure of Revelation was provided by the use of the Hallel Psalms (113–18) in chapter 19, immediately preceding the "marriage supper of the Lamb". The association of these Hallel Psalms with the Jewish festivals, and in particular with Passover, suggested at first that this chapter reflected the Paschal Eucharist of the Church. By working backwards through the book from this point, we became convinced that an entire Paschal liturgy could be reconstructed. And this in turn fits in with the Seer's statement that his vision was experienced "on the Lord's day" (1: 10). More will be said later regarding the meaning of the Lord's day. Suffice it to say for the present that the phrase—which first appears in Christian literature in this place—may refer not only to Sunday, but also to the Pascha or to the Parousia. The overlapping of images and symbols, double and even triple meanings to words and phrases, is not uncommon in the Apocalypse, a device not unknown by any means to the author of the Gospel of John.

At the outset, however, a simple *caveat* needs to be made. It is very tempting to liturgiologists to read back into early sources the liturgical developments of a later period. In the case of the Apocalypse specifically, the richness of ceremonial and symbolism depicted in the heavenly

---

[1] *A Rebirth of Images, The Making of St. John's Apocalypse*, 1949.
[2] *A Critical and Exegetical Commentary on the Revelation of St. John* (International Critical Commentary), 2 vols., 1920.

worship of chapters 4–5 may not be a literal reflection of the actual state of Christian worship at the time Revelation was written, but rather a source of inspiration and suggestion for embellishments of the Church's liturgy that were developed in later times. At least, this has been the general view of most commentators. Hence the charge may very well be made against the present thesis that a Paschal liturgy of a later age has been read into the Apocalypse, not read out of it. The problem of a right interpretation at this point is certainly a real one, and one that ought to be faced honestly.

We readily admit that it would be very difficult, if not impossible, to construct from the Apocalypse an order of Paschal celebration, if we did not have the outline of such an order in the *Apostolic Tradition* of Hippolytus, a work composed about a century later than Revelation. In our exposition of Hippolytus' rite in Part One, we have attempted to show the extent to which Hippolytus' claim that his rite is truly "apostolic" can be justified. We need not repeat the arguments again. We have suggested that, apart from certain details of ceremonial, there is nothing in the general *ordo* of the Paschal rite described by Hippolytus that could not have been in use in the first century. It is not unreasonable to suppose that the broad outline of the Paschal liturgy known to Hippolytus (and independently to Tertullian) may have obtained in churches so well established and developed as those of Asia at the close of the first century.

There is a major fallacy, we believe, in the tacit assumption of so many New Testament critics that the worship of the primitive Church must necessarily have been so rudimentary as that described in the summary of Acts 2: 46–7, or so chaotic as that observed by the disorderly community at Corinth against which St. Paul protested with considerable vigor. Christian worship was not a thing invented *de novo*, but was constructed out of forms inherited from Judaism that were highly ceremonious, orderly, and disciplined. We know enough about the liturgies of the Temple, the synagogue, and the domestic rites such as the Passover—and, not least, of the rites of sectarian groups such as those revealed in the Qumran scrolls—to recognize a cultic inheritance of Christianity that was carefully regulated, basically traditional, and pre-eminently decorous.

So much, indeed, has been universally admitted with respect to the liturgical materials in the First Epistle of Clement, a document exactly contemporaneous with the Apocalypse. The freedom of charismatic inspiration in primitive Christian worship had to do with the content of song, prayer, and prophecy. In the sphere of "order"—what we may call structural patterns—the Church's liturgy was in the main in keeping with Jewish tradition. The Apocalypse, therefore, should not be viewed, in matters liturgical, as "ahead of its time", but as a faithful witness to the usages of its own day and age.

The basic pattern of the Apocalypse is a very simple one. Its prophecy unfolds in a series of sevens: the seven letters of the seven churches, the seven seals, the seven trumpets, the seven vials. Yet at certain places there are pauses or interludes that seem to interrupt this sequence:

(1) Chapters 4 and 5 are not so much an interlude—for the sequence of the seven letters is uninterrupted—as they are a preparation and setting for the opening of the seven seals.

(2) Chapter 7 is inserted between the opening of the sixth and of the seventh seals, and recounts, in a liturgical framework similar to chapters 4 and 5, the sealing of the 144,000 of the sons of Israel.

(3) Chapters 10: 1—11: 13 form the next interlude, placed between the sixth and the seventh trumpets. It recounts the prophecy of the two witnesses contained in the "little scroll". The blast of the seventh trumpet (11: 15) inaugurates a third Woe and the beginning of the seven vials of wrath. But the interlude is prolonged, after this blast, to the end of chapter 15. This interlude also contains liturgical materials.

With the conclusion of the seventh vial, the Apocalypse ends in paeans of victory: the song of triumph over the fall of Babylon (chapter 18); the Hallel psalmody and the marriage supper of the Lamb (chapter 19); and the vision of the world to come (chapters 20–2).

What is immediately striking about this pattern is the pause that occurs between the sixth and seventh members of the series of seals and trumpets, and also in a real sense that of the vials. This is done in such a way that the seventh and concluding item of each series is made identical with the first item of the succeeding series. The only exception is the initial series of seven letters. Dr. Farrer is surely correct in seeing this numerology of six-pause-seven = one as symbolic of the Christian week. The seventh of the series, which represents the Jewish Sabbath, is held over, to be replaced by the first (or octave) of a new series, namely the Christian Sunday. This symbolism of seven-eight = one we have already had occasion to note in Chapter 1.[1] We shall not repeat what was there brought forward, except to call attention to the

[1] See above, pp. 20–21.

explicit acceptance and use by the Seer of the Apocalypse of the millenarian scheme regarding creation, history, and final end, in 20: 2-7. The world will last 6,000 years, corresponding to the six days of creation. A millennium of 1,000 years will then follow, during which the saints of the first resurrection will reign in peace with Christ—a kind of seventh day of rest. Then Satan will be loosed, the ultimate conflict will be set on the earth, followed immediately by the second resurrection, final judgment, and inauguration of the world to come that shall last without end.

We possess, incidentally, the explicit testimony of Irenaeus that this millenarian teaching was a cardinal doctrine among the disciples of the Seer such as Papias.[1] And it is interesting to note that the learned Roman presbyter Gaius, who flourished in the latter part of the second century, attributed the Apocalypse to the heretic Cerinthus on grounds of this millenarian teaching. For he could not be persuaded that an "apostle" subscribed to such a doctrine.[2]

We are thus in a position to understand the clue, rich in its overtones of meaning, provided by the Seer himself in dating his visions and prophecy on "the Lord's day" (1: 10). This is the earliest occurrence of the phrase in Christian literature. Its obvious meaning is Sunday—at least, since his time it is a commonplace among Christians for the name of the first day of the week.[3] Yet there is no necessary reason why the Seer may not also have meant the "Day of the Lord", the Parousia, for his prophecy leads to climactic conclusion with the Second Coming of Christ.[4] But the connection between Sunday and Parousia, the first and the octave day, is provided by the Pascha, since it is the resurrection of Christ that provides for Christian faith significance to both Sunday and Parousia. Thus, as we have already seen, by the second century at the latest, the Pascha was the normal occasion in the Church for the ministration of baptismal initiation, by which the convert was mystically conjoined with Christ in death and resurrection and given the promise of eternal life in the world to come.

All this complex of associated meanings is more than hinted in the words of the Seer that lead up to the revelation on "the Lord's day".

---

[1] *Adv. Haer.* v, 33, 3-4; cf. also v, 28, 3.
[2] Eusebius *H.E.*, iii, 28.
[3] See above, p. 18, note 1.
[4] This interpretation was favored by F. J. A. Hort, *The Apocalypse of St. John I–III*, 1908.

> ... from Jesus Christ, the faithful witness
> the firstborn of the dead,
> and the archon of the kings of the earth.
>
> To him who loved us and loosed us
> from our sins in his blood,
> and made us a kingdom,
> priests to God and his Father ...
>
> Behold, he comes with the clouds ...

The phrases of these verses (1: 5–7) weave together in unmistakable fashion the historic redemptive act in Christ's death, resurrection and ascension, the Christian experience of salvation in the forgiveness of sins and incorporation into Christ's kingdom and priesthood, and the certain expectation of Christ's coming again in glory. The themes of Pascha and Parousia could not be more intimately bound together. Nor is it irrelevant to note the variant reading in verse 5—λούσαντι for λύσαντι—a later ecclesiastical commentary, no doubt, that more closely identified the "loosing" from sin with the "washing" of Baptism.[1]

One should note, too, the close relationship here of the thought of the Apocalypse and of the Gospel of John—whatever view one might take of the identity or relation of the authors of the two writings. The Passion narrative of the Gospel of John begins "six days before the Passover" (12: 1). On the sixth day the Lamb is slain; the powers of evil under the prince of this world wreak their worst upon Him. Yet the death of the Lamb is in fact the crucial point of His triumph and the exhibition of His true glory, which after the pause of the seventh day of rest in the tomb, is made manifest in the resurrection on the first day of the week. From the victory of Christ on the Cross flows the stream of water and blood, the Paschal sacraments, by which the Christian appropriates to himself participation in that victory. The realized eschatology of the Fourth Gospel is at one with the millenarian eschatology of the Apocalypse. It is only the imagery that is different. The Gospel employs the commemorative narrative of the Pascha; the Revelation relates the theme in the apocalyptic symbolism of the Parousia. Both the Evangelist and the Seer give their testimony from the vantage point of experience of the Paschal liturgy of the Asian churches.[2]

[1] See note of Charles, *op. cit.*, I, 15–16, particularly the references to 1 Cor. 6: 11, Eph. 5: 26, Titus 3: 5, Heb. 10:22.

[2] There may be certain implications here for the relation of the Johannine writings to Quartodecimanism. Whatever may be the connection of the gospel

We are now ready to show a synoptic correlation of the structure of the Apocalypse with the outline of the Paschal liturgy—what constitutes our one thesis in these pages:

The Scrutinies	The Seven Letters	Rev. 1–3
The Vigil	The Assembly before the Throne of God	4–5
(a) The Lessons	The Seals, I–VI	6
The Initiation	The Pause: Sealing of the White-robed Martyrs	7
The Synaxis	The Seventh Seal	8
(a) The Prayers	The censing	
(b) The Law (Exodus)	The Trumpets, I–VI = The Woes, I–II	8–9
(c) The Prophets	The Pause: The Little Scroll; the Two Witnesses	10–11
(d) The Gospel	The Seventh Trumpet = The Third Woe: The Struggle of Christ and Antichrist	12–15
	The Vials, I–VII	16–18
(e) The Psalmody	The Hallelujah	19
The Eucharist	The Marriage Supper of the Lamb	19
	The Consummation	20–2

It must be emphasized once again that we do not suppose that the Apocalypse is a Paschal liturgy. It might conceivably be viewed as a commentary upon that liturgy from the vantage point of prophecy. But we do not even insist on this. We mean only to propose that the Paschal liturgy has suggested to the Seer a structural pattern for the presentation of his message. His primary interest was certainly not liturgy, though his book is full of liturgical pieces. Neither are the sources of his imagery derived from the liturgy, except in so far as certain passages, such as the Exodus narrative, were part and parcel of the liturgical ritual of the Pascha with which he was familiar.

And it must be readily admitted that the Seer has drawn upon other structural patterns than those of the liturgy. The sevenfold schematization has its basis in the Christian week, no doubt. But there may well be other influences that have contributed to the author's preference for

with it (see above, p. 45, note 1), the Apocalypse—if our theory of its Paschal structure is sound—does not give support to the Quartodecimans. It will be recalled that Polycrates of Ephesus appealed for his Quartodeciman tradition to the gospel, and not to the Apocalypse.

it, as opposed, for example, to a threefold or a ninefold or tenfold system of enumeration. To cite but one notable instance—there is the awkward attempt to integrate the scheme of seven trumpets with a scheme of three woes. Most commentators seek to work out this difficulty by resort to source analysis. In this endeavour they may well be right. We are not concerned here with that fascinating subject of "sources". The problem is further complicated by the fact that the plagues brought about by the seven trumpets, or at least the first five of them, are obviously based upon the plagues upon Egypt recounted in Exodus 7–11. But there were ten plagues upon Egypt, not three, or five, or seven.

This example by itself is sufficient to show that the Seer, in adopting the liturgy as a general framework, was not impelled to follow it in every detail, or even inspired to write a full commentary upon it. The liturgy does not provide a clue to all the wealth of content in the Revelation. Students must continue to search the Scriptures—and many other sources—for their exegesis of these remarkable visions. All that the present discussion aims to show is that the Paschal liturgy gave the Seer a basic focus of reference, both for the major theme of his prophecy and for the larger outline through which it was conveyed to the churches.

VII

THE SCRUTINIES, VIGIL, AND INITIATION

(A) THE SCRUTINIES

THE LETTERS to the seven churches—representative of all types of churches—provide a preface to the Apocalypse proper. They consist of warnings, admonitions, judgments, encouragements, and promises, and are filled with exhortations to repentance and endurance. Designed to screen the members of the churches for the "baptism by fire" of the coming great Day, these letters are a summons to pass muster for the approaching ordeal of death and resurrection. The half-hearted, negligent, and nominally committed are warned of their perilous situation; and in particular, every root of Judaism, paganism, and heresy is placed under judgment of condemnation.

Why the Seer adopted an epistolary form for his preface to the visions is not our concern here. What is germane to our purpose is the suggestion these letters give to the screening of candidates for Baptism in the weeks or days immediately prior to the initiatory rites of the Pascha. The institution of the catechumenate appears to have developed in the churches sometime during the second century. Already by the time of Hippolytus it is formalized and established. We have seen how he describes the instructions, exorcisms, and examinations, leading to the final screening of the candidates by the bishop on the eve of the Pascha;[1] the ceremonies that later came to be known as "scrutinies".

In his Homilies delivered at Caesarea, Origen frequently reminded the catechumens of the moral requirements for admission to Baptism:

You who desire to receive holy Baptism and be deserving of the grace of the Spirit, must first be purged from the Law, and then by hearing God's word cut away the roots of vices and correct your barbarous and wild manners, so that you may be able, after having learned meekness and humility, to receive the grace of the Holy Spirit.[2]

[1] See above, p. 52.
[2] *Hom. in Lev.* vi, 2; also see *Hom. in Luc.* xxi and xxii. Cf. Jean Daniélou, *Origen*, 1955, pp. 54-5.

In his Apology *Against Celsus*, he specifically mentions two classes of catechumens: (1) the beginners, who are receiving elementary instruction and have not yet received the sign that they have been purified; and (2) those who are ready for initiation, whose lives are being carefully examined as to their fitness. Among the latter, some are wholeheartedly accepted; others, whose secret sins are discovered, are driven out of the community of the Church.[1]

It is interesting to note that, as late as the middle of the fourth century, Cyril of Jerusalem speaks of the exorcisms of catechumens as a cleansing of the soul, and links them closely with the candidates' need for "saving penitence". In particular, he compares the catechizings to a receiving of armor "against heresies, against Jews and Samaritans and Gentiles," in order that the candidates may overcome "the powers that oppose" them and "escape defeat from every heretical attempt".[2]

The promises offered by the Seer of the Apocalypse to those who endure steadfastly through the approaching crisis are worth noting, for their interesting combination of both sacramental and eschatological *motifs*:

2:7 (Ephesus): I will grant to eat of the tree of life that is in the paradise of God.

2:10-11 (Smyrna): I will give you the crown of life . . . He shall not be harmed by the second death.

2:17 (Pergamum): I will grant of the hidden manna, and I will grant to him a white stone, with a new name written upon the stone that no one knows except him who receives it.

[Note that Hippolytus refers to the secret given to the baptized as "the white stone of which John said that there is a new name written upon it which no man knows except him who receives it".[3]]

2:26, 28 (Thyatira): I will give him power over the nations . . . I will give him the morning Star.

3:5 (Sardis): He shall be clad in white garments . . . I will confess his name before my Father and before his angels.

3:12 (Philadelphia): I will make him a pillar in the temple of my God . . . I will write on him the name of my God, and the name of the city of my God, the new Jerusalem that comes down from heaven from my God, and my new name.

3:20-1 (Laodicea): I will come to him and sup with him, and he with me . . . I will give to him to sit with me on my throne.

This last promise is of particular significance, for it both recalls the

[1] iii, 51.
[2] See the *Protocatechesis* (ed. F. L. Cross), sections 9-10.
[3] *Apostolic Tradition* xxiii, 14 (ed. Dix, p. 43).

saying of Jesus at the Last Supper—"that you may eat and drink at my table in my kingdom, and sit upon thrones . . ." (Luke 22: 30)—and looks forward to the climactic marriage supper of the Lamb at the conclusion of the Seer's visions.

We have remarked that the seven letters, unlike the later unfolding visions, contain no pause or interlude between the sixth and seventh members of the series. We would suggest that the Paschal ceremonies give the clue to this peculiarity. As the symbol of the scrutinies, the letters in this liturgical sequence belong to the pre-baptismal stage, the old order of pre-Christian life. So they represent the week of seven days, not the octave. The Paschal liturgy proper begins only with chapter 4, the assembly of the people for the Vigil, Initiation, and Eucharist. All that precedes the Paschal liturgy is preparation, and lies in the pre-redemptive cycle of time.

(B) THE VIGIL

Chapters 4 and 5 of Revelation have been so frequently studied by liturgiologists that there is little need here for more than a few summary remarks. The *mise en scène* is the throne-room of heaven, which is also a temple with an altar. The imagery is without question built out of Isaiah 6, Ezekiel 1, and Daniel 7. But it is not fanciful to see here also an idealized meeting place and assembly of the Church, with its cathedra for the bishop,[1] the seats of the elders on either side, the deacons standing before the throne, and the holy Table with the Scriptural scroll or book. The arrangement conforms to everything we know about the ordering of ancient Christian congregations at their worship.

The fact that the setting is both throne-room and temple-shrine, where Christ the Lamb is the central figure, links the scene with the Seer's assertion that in Christ the redeemed have been made a kingdom and priests to God the Father. We must not, however, take the twenty-four elders and the seven spirits (*i.e.*, the deacons) as necessarily corresponding in number to the elders and deacons of the Seer's church in Asia. Other factors have entered into this number-symbolism. Here we have an example of how the imagery of Revelation has itself tended to shape later usages, in particular the number of clergy of the church at Rome.[2]

The Seer lays his scene in heaven, not in an earthly church, because

---

[1] Cf. the way Ignatius speaks of the bishop as a symbol of God the Father: *Mag.* 3, 1; 6, 1; 13, 2; *Trall.* 3, 1; *Smyr.* 8, 1.

[2] Cf. Cornelius of Rome in Eusebius *H.E.* vi, 43, 11.

heaven is the sphere of the mighty conflict of which his prophecy tells. But it also reveals the ancient Christian view that the worship of the earthly Church is at one with the worship of the hosts of heaven—that it is lifted up by Christ's ascension in union with angels and archangels and all the company of heaven. So we would understand the introduction in all the liturgies of the *Sursum corda* and *Sanctus*.

It is possible that the anthems in these chapters reflect a custom of introit hymnody or psalmody in the liturgy, though there is no evidence for this in any of the ancient liturgies before the latter part of the fourth century.[1] More important for our purpose is the sealed scroll, which only the Lamb can unseal, and whose meaning only He can make plain. For it is the unsealing of this scroll that opens the first major series of visions of the Seer.

The sealed scroll is undoubtedly, as Miss Mowry has so persuasively argued, a copy of the Old Testament Torah.[2] The Scriptures of the Old Covenant, their revelations and promises, can be properly understood only by reference to Christ. This viewpoint is a commonplace of early Christian apologetic. It underlies Luke-Acts, and the Gospel of John; it is specifically stated by Ignatius, pseudo-Barnabas, Justin Martyr, and others.[3]

We have already noted that, in the later liturgies, the Paschal vigil consisted of the reading of the Old Testament lections from the Law and the Prophets, with instruction and homiletic interpretation.[4] As the first six seals of the scroll are opened—down to the pause that comes before the breaking of the seventh seal—we have a series of apocalyptic predictions. Dr. R. H. Charles has demonstrated that these predictions, both in their order and contents, correspond exactly to the Little Apocalypse of Mark 13, and its parallels in the other Synoptic gospels.[5] The series in Revelation 6: 1—7: 1 consists of:

---

[1] The whole subject of psalmody and hymnody in the primitive Eucharist needs more careful study, for the silence of Justin on this subject ought not to be glossed over. Even so, the oldest references have to do with psalmody between the lessons, not to introit psalmody. See the pertinent and suggestive comments of B. Fischer, *Die Psalmenfrömmigkeit der Märtyrerkirche*, 1949, especially pp. 2–3.

[2] L. Mowry, "Revelation 4–5 and Early Christian Liturgical Usage", *JBL* LXXI, 1952, pp. 82–3.

[3] *E.g.*, Luke 24: 27, 44–5; Acts 8: 35, 17: 2–3; John 5: 39–47; Ignatius *Phil.* 8, 2; Barnabas 2, 4, and throughout the argument of the epistle to ch. 18; Justin *Dial.* 11 ff.

[4] See above, p. 55

[5] *Op. cit.*, I, 158–9.

1. War
2. International strife
3. Famine
4. Pestilence
5. Persecution
6. Earthquakes and cosmic signs

We have to do here with traditional materials. We also recall that the apocalyptic section in the Gospel of Mark immediately precedes the Passion narrative, and is structured in a time-sequence of three-hour intervals that suggests liturgical use.[1]

The correspondence is a striking one. And it would not seem to be stretching the evidence to suggest that the Paschal celebration at Rome in the first century, as denoted by Mark, was comparable to the Paschal celebration of the Asian churches of the same period in this respect. The vigil was devoted to reading and interpretation of apocalyptic and prophetic material. To the Christian mind of that age it would not seem strange to use apocalyptic as a key to unlock the mysteries hidden in the Old Testament. Apocalyptic was the last great flowering of Jewish prophecy before and immediately concurrent with the rise of Christianity. Not only the Gospels but St. Paul testify to its popularity, not to speak of the impact on early Christian writing of non-canonical apocalypses such as Enoch, Baruch, the Testament of Levi, and Second Esdras. The Book of Revelation is only one, albeit the most notable, example of the vogue of apocalyptic in the churches of Asia Minor, which finally issued in the Montanist schism.

(C) THE INITIATION

The pause that follows the breaking of the sixth seal gives place to the "sealing" of the servants of God upon their foreheads: "These are they who have come out of the great tribulation, and have washed their robes and made them white in the blood of the Lamb" (7: 14). The Seer is speaking here literally of the martyrs—probably Jewish-Christian martyrs, who have received the baptism of blood. But Christian Baptism is a baptism into the death of Christ. In "Johannine" theology water and blood go together. We may legitimately see in this pause, therefore, the initiation ceremony of washing and sealing in the Paschal liturgy.

[1] See above, pp. 34–5.

The concept of sealing was a rich one in the metaphors and applications of early Christian writers. Its meanings have been thoroughly canvassed by F. J. Dölger,[1] and more recently, in so far as it is applied to Christian initiation, by Professor G. W. H. Lampe.[2] The sealing, in the sense of branding with a name or sign of an owner, underlies the term in Revelation 7: 3, and recalls at once a similar use of the word in the Pauline epistles where the association of ideas is definitely linked with the recalling of the Christian's initiation.[3] In Revelation 14: 1, the seal on the forehead is specifically said to be the name of the Lamb and of the Father. Surely this circumstance is intended to remind the hearer of the divine Name said over him at his baptism—inwardly and invisibly manifested in the spirit of Christian character, so that in the great tribulation the Lord knows them that belong to Him.

Another passage to note is the anthem in 7: 15–17, since it is constructed from ideas and phrases in Psalms 23, 42, and 121. The first two of these psalms were especially associated in the ancient liturgies with the baptismal rite.[4] To what extent, however, the seventh chapter of Revelation betrays a knowledge of all the initiatory ceremonies recounted by Hippolytus and Tertullian, must be left an open question. We may well be dealing here (as in the case of the number of the elders and deacons) with influences which the Apocalypse itself has had upon the development of the baptismal rites. But at least these aspects of the ceremonial and ritual seem to be implied:

1. The renunciation of Satan
2. The profession of faith
3. The washing

---

[1] *Sphragis* (Studien zur Geschichte und Kultur des Altertums, V, 3–4; 1911).

[2] *The Seal of the Spirit*, 1951.

[3] 2 Cor. 1: 22; Eph. 1: 13, 4: 30.

[4] For Psalm 23, see J. Quasten, "The Painting of the Good Shepherd at Dura-Europos", *Mediaeval Studies*, IX, 1947, pp. 1–18, and his earlier study on the same theme: "Das Bild des Guten Hirten in den altchristlichen Baptisterien und in den Taufliturgien des Ostens und des Westens", *Pisciculi F. J. Dölger dargeboten*, 1939, pp. 220–44. Cf. also L. De Bruyne, "La décoration des baptistères paléochrétiens", *Miscellanea liturgica in honorem L. Cuniberti Mohlberg* (Bibliotheca "Ephemerides Liturgicae" 22), 1948, I, especially pp. 197–203.

For Psalm 42: Augustine *Enarr. in Ps. XLI*, 1; cf. the deer drinking from the streams in the apse mosaic of the Lateran Basilica in Rome—the cathedral church of the city, where the baptistery was located. Psalm 42 is still used in the Roman rite of Easter and Whitsun Eves for the procession to the baptistery before the Blessing of the Font.

4. The sealing with the Name
5. The investment with white garments

It is possible, too, that the sealing carries further recollection of the chrismation and laying on of hands in "Confirmation". But this cannot be so definitely read out of the text.

VIII

THE SYNAXIS AND EUCHARIST

WITH CHAPTER 8, the Seer's visions move into a new series: the plagues let loose by the angels with the seven trumpets. The series is preceded by the opening of the seventh seal, the half-hour silence in heaven, and the offering up of the prayers of all the saints as it were incense. The transition is in some ways an awkward one, but the problems are mainly literary, and we may therefore leave them to the literary critics. In any event, the breaking of the seventh seal produces silence rather than turmoil, prayer rather than forces of destruction. It is a kind of sabbath rest that marks a final conclusion to the old order of the seven-fold week, yet at the same time suggests the emergence of the new order of the octave that begins with the trumpets.

Liturgically, this pause may be either the silent prayers of the faithful as they conclude their vigil and await the return of the newly baptized to the assembly; or it may actually be the so-called Prayers of the Faithful of the liturgy itself. We prefer the former explanation. For there is no evidence from the later liturgies that the Prayers of the Faithful—intercessory prayers, after the pattern of the prayers of the Good Friday rite of the Roman Missal[1]—came at the beginning of the synaxis, but rather at its conclusion, immediately before the Offertory of the Eucharist. It is likely that the pause of prayer here is a necessary delay required after the initiations in the baptistery,[2] until the time when all the people could be re-assembled with the clergy. During this pause, the faithful who awaited the return of the baptized and the clergy would devote themselves to earnest prayer.[3]

(A) THE SYNAXIS

The ancient synaxis of the liturgy, before the elaborations of the

[1] See the discussion of their form in G. Dix, *The Shape of the Liturgy*, 1945, pp. 41-4.

[2] See above, p. 56, note 4.

[3] The descriptions of the Vigils at Jerusalem in the *Pilgrimage* of Etheria (late fourth century) suggest periods of silent "watch" by the people.

fourth century, consisted of lessons from the Scriptures, interspersed possibly with some psalmody,[1] and a sermon. After the dismissal of the unbaptized, the synaxis concluded with the Prayers of the Faithful, following which without break came the Eucharist. It is only fair to state at this point that there is no evidence extant from the ante-Nicene period that the synaxis formed part of the Paschal rite. Hippolytus ignores it altogether. Justin describes it for an ordinary Sunday liturgy, but likewise implies, in his description of the baptismal ceremonies, that the synaxis was replaced by the vigil and initiations. The later liturgies, however, did include a synaxis before the Easter Eucharist, after the vigil and baptisms had been completed. At Jerusalem the testimony of Etheria in her famous *Pilgrimage* is not precise, but the old Armenian lectionary that preserves the Jerusalem custom contains lessons and psalms for the synaxis.[2] Both the Byzantine and the Roman liturgies have an Epistle, Gradual, and Gospel for the Easter eucharistic rite.

We cannot affirm, of course, that at so early a time as the end of the first century the liturgies of the churches had developed a fixed pattern of lessons for the synaxis. The number doubtless varied, depending upon the wishes of the celebrant. Justin mentions only two at the Sunday synaxis, one from the Gospels and one from the Prophets. But his remarks are not so precise as to warrant the conclusion that only two readings were invariably selected from these books. The oldest strata of the later liturgies, both of the East and of the West, contain three: Old Testament, Epistle, and Gospel. The late fourth-century liturgy of the *Apostolic Constitutions*—an ideal liturgy, probably never used as such—provided for five (viii, 5): Law, Prophets, Epistles, Acts, Gospels. It is possible that the Psalms, if employed between the lessons, were originally accounted as lections rather than as hymns.[3] These readings of the synaxis were derived by the Church from the synagogue, whose liturgy included lections from the Law and the Prophets.

We have constructed the synaxis underlying Revelation 8–18 in a pattern of three lessons: Law, Prophets, and Gospel, with psalmody before and after the gospel. Of course, we are aware that the Book of Revelation was composed before there was a New Testament canon. The Bible of the Seer was the Old Testament. From the synagogue he would be familiar with the readings from the Law and the Prophets. But we need not by any means exclude the reading of Christian books

[1] See above, p. 88, note 1.
[2] F. C. Conybeare, *Rituale Armenorum*, 1905, pp. 518–21.
[3] See above, p. 88, note 1.

from the Church's worship so late as the end of the first century.

Paul expected his letters to be read at the assembly of his churches.[1] The gospels, even if they were not composed to serve as lectionaries, were certainly familiar to Christians from hearing them read in worship.[2] We possess evidence from Hermas that Christian prophecies were allowed to be read at the Church's synaxes,[3] and this testimony is almost exactly contemporaneous with the Apocalypse. Hence a sequence of Law-Prophets-Gospel in the synaxis of the Asian churches at the close of the first century is a perfectly reasonable hypothesis—provided we do not interpret "gospel" in too narrow a sense. It might be any Christian book that interpreted the gospel, such as Revelation itself, or some similar prophetic work, no less than one written in "gospel" form. The Synoptic gospels contain apocalyptic prophecies. The so-called Q source has the character of a prophetic work.[4] Even an epistle such as Hebrews might be viewed as a "gospel", for it is a treatise or instruction upon a major gospel theme.

The plan of the synaxis section of the Book of Revelation may be outlined as follows:

The Law	The Seven Trumpets:	
	1. Hail	
	2. Sea of Blood	
	3. Bitter Waters	
	4. Darkening of Sun and Moon	
	5. Locusts	= First Woe
	6. Army	= Second Woe
The Prophets	The Pause:	
	The Little Scroll	
	The Two Witnesses	
The Gospel	7. The Antichrist ⎫	= Third Woe
	The Seven Vials ⎭	
	1. Sores	
	2. Sea of Blood	
	3. Rivers of Blood	

[1] Cf. Col. 4: 15.

[2] See above, p. 27, notes 1 and 2. I have attempted to show that the author of the Epistle of James was familiar with Matthew from hearing the gospel read in church; see "The Epistle of James and the Gospel of Matthew", *JBL* LXXV, 1956, pp. 40–51.

[3] *Vis.* ii, 4, 3.

[4] Cf. B. H. Streeter's essay in W. Sanday (ed.), *Studies in the Synoptic Problem*, 1911, pp. 141–64.

4. Scorching Heat
5. Darkness
6. Kings from the East
7. Fall of Babylon

Certain general observations about these two series, of Trumpets and of Vials, occur at once. There is an obvious relationship in the character of the two series of plagues, more so than between these two series and the plagues of the seven Seals. For these two are intimately linked by the work of the Antichrist, let loose by the seventh Trumpet to carry over his deadly work in the plagues produced by the Vials.

The plagues of the seven Trumpets are unmistakably based upon the Exodus narrative—at least, the first six of them that occur before the pause for the prophecy of the Little Scroll. The plagues of the seven Vials, however, are not drawn so directly from the Exodus narrative, though they grow out of and develop some of their themes. It is the struggle with the Antichrist that principally links the two series. And the account of this struggle is the "gospel" message of the Seer. It is "the eternal gospel" (14: 6). The plagues of the Vials are the fulfilment of the plagues of the Trumpets, in the same way that the Gospel is the fulfilment of the promise of the Law.

Between the Law (the Trumpets) and the Gospel (the Vials) comes the intermezzo of the Little Scroll in chapters 10: 1—11: 14. We would identify this section with the lesson from the Prophets, though we are not concerned here either with the problem of the Seer's sources for this section, or with the exact interpretation of this interlude. The Two Witnesses (11: 4 ff.), about whose identification so many theories have been advanced, seem to us to be clearly related by the Seer—whoever else they may represent for him— to Moses and Elijah. These men are the type-figures of the Law and the Prophets that lead to Christ, as in the Transfiguration pericope of the gospels. The prophecy of the Two Witnesses is followed by a second prophecy of the persecution of the Woman (i.e., the Church) by the Dragon. Between these two prophecies there is an anthem (11: 15-19). And at the conclusion of the second prophecy there comes another anthem, introduced and identified as the Song of Moses and the Song of the Lamb (15: 2-4).

The first of these anthems is based on Psalm 2, one of the Messianic psalms of the ancient Church, considered as a prophecy of the Passion and Resurrection of Christ.[1] It is therefore most appropriate in the context of a Paschal liturgy, and especially so in relation to a prophetic

[1] Acts 4: 25, 13: 33; cf. Rom. 1: 4; 1 Peter 1: 3; Heb. 1: 5, 5: 5.

lesson, for the Psalter was itself a prophetic book of the Christ.[1] The second anthem recalls Exodus 15, a very natural selection for a Paschal liturgy. This song is still used in the Roman liturgy of Easter Even as a canticle after the Exodus lesson of the Vigil.

The synaxis concludes, after the Gospel proclamation of the triumph of Christ over Antichrist, with the Hallelujah psalmody of chapter 19: 1–8, which serves as a responsory to the great paean of victory over the fall of Babylon. The Hallel psalms sung by the Jews at their great feasts were Psalms 113–18. The citation of 113: 1 and 115: 13 in 19: 5 is unmistakable. Indeed, if there is one certain link between the liturgy of Judaism and the liturgy of the Church, it is the use of the Hallel psalms at the Paschal celebration.[2]

In the later liturgies the Alleluia chant played a great role. In some rites the Alleluia-psalmody came before, in others it came after the Gospel lesson. In all extant rites except the Mozarabic liturgy of Spain it now comes before the Gospel. But this may be due to what happened, for example, in the Roman rite, when the lessons were reduced to two. The psalm chants were combined in one place, and put between the Epistle and the Gospel. This is why, in the Roman liturgy, the two chants of Gradual and Alleluia follow each other immediately.[3]

If we were to reconstruct the actual rite underlying the synaxis section of Revelation (chapters 8–19), we should therefore come to some such "proper" of the liturgy as follows:

> The Law: Exodus 7–14
> The Prophets: Unknown, but probably included Daniel 7
> Psalm 2
> Exodus 15, The Song of Moses
> The Gospel: The Final Judgment
> Alleluia: Psalms 113 ff.

(B) THE EUCHARIST

The Hallel psalms lead directly into the invitation to "the marriage supper of the Lamb", and the visions of the Lamb, the Word of God, and His Bride, the Church of the Heavenly Jerusalem. The consummation of the Paschal liturgy is the eucharistic banquet in the presence

---

[1] See above, p. 88, note 1.

[2] These Psalms occur in all the ancient liturgies in the propers for Easter and Easter week. Their use at the Jewish Passover is attested in the Mishnah, *Pesachim* x, 5–7.

[3] Cf. J. A. Jungmann, *The Mass of the Roman Rite*, I, 1951, pp. 395–6, 423–5.

of Christ, as He holds intimate communion with His Church, giving it light and life. One needs only to recall the gospel parables of the Messianic banquet,[1] and the kingdom sayings of the Lord at the Last Supper, to realize the eucharistic associations of the great eschatological theme of the Seer's supper of the Lamb. As in chapters 4–5, the worship of the Church on earth is really a participation in and an anticipation of the worship of heaven.

The Eucharist is the earnest of the final consummation of the age to come. This theme has been so ably presented by New Testament and liturgical scholars that it needs no detailed exposition here. Our purpose is achieved if we have succeeded in demonstrating that a very real clue to the basic structure of Revelation is to be found in the Paschal liturgy of the Church. For this liturgy, let us repeat, is the Christian experience of the gospel of redemption from sin, Satan, and death, in the victorious triumph of Christ our Passover.

[1] Cf. C. H. Dodd, *The Parables of the Kingdom*, 1935, pp. 55–6, 120–2.

INDEX